Carving Teddy Bears

with Kelley Stadelman

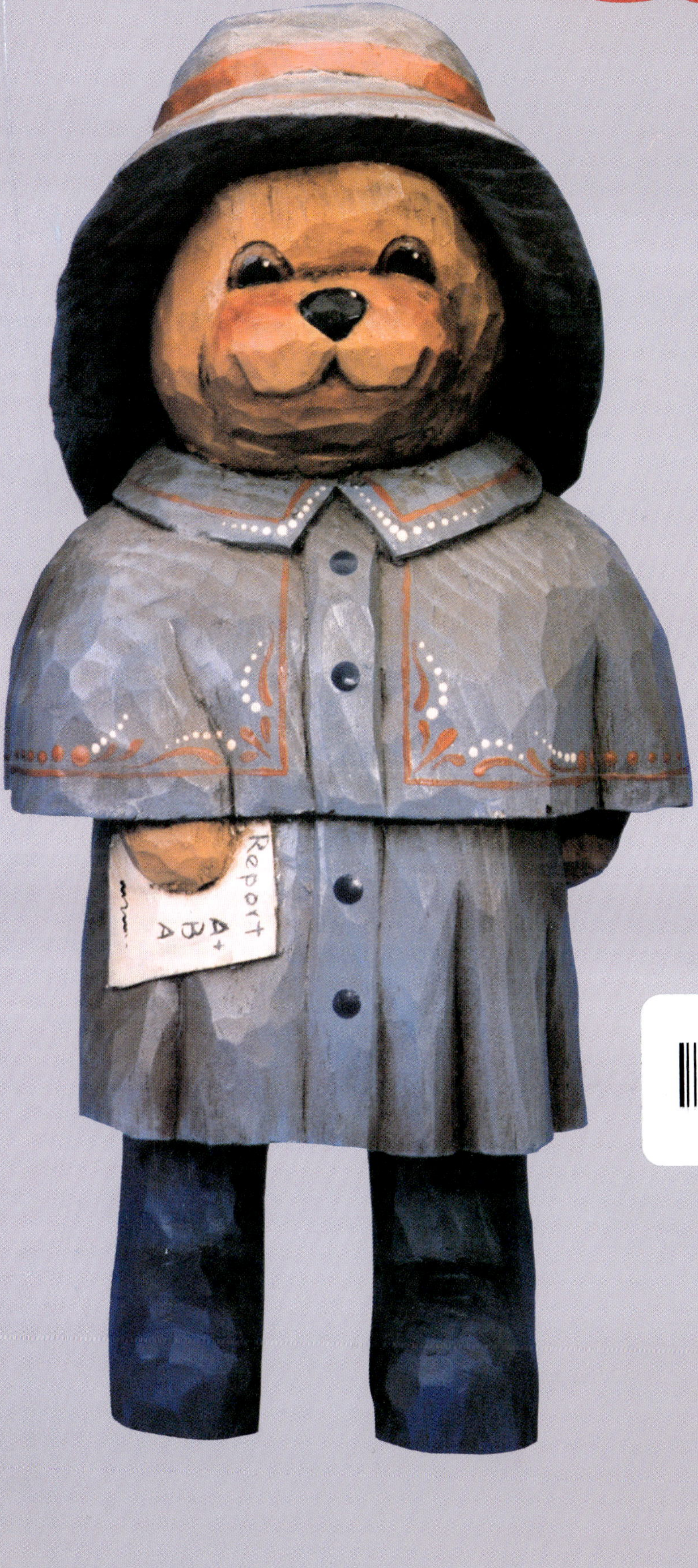

Text written with and photography by Douglas Congdon-Martin

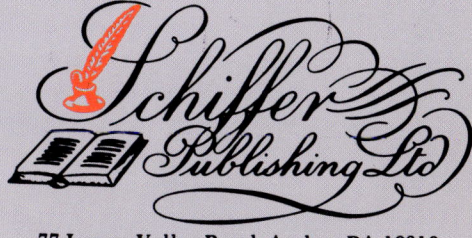

77 Lower Valley Road, Atglen, PA 19310

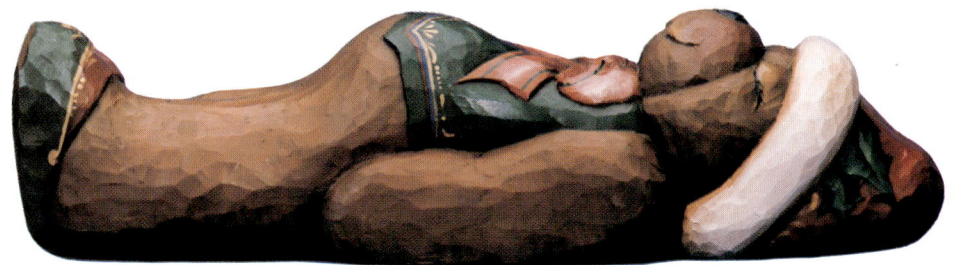

Copyright © 1996 by Kelley Stadelman

All rights reserved. No part of this work may be reproduced or used in any form or by any means--graphic, electronic, or mechanical, including photocopying or information storage and retrieval systems--without written permission from the copyright holder.

This book is meant only for personal home use and recreation. It is not intended for commercial applications or manufacturing purposes.

Printed in China

ISBN: 0-88740-890-7

BOOK DESIGN BY AUDREY L. WHITESIDE

Library of Congress Cataloging-in-Publication Data

Stadelman, Kelley.
   Carving teddy bears with Kelley Stadelman.
     p.   cm.
   ISBN 0-88740-890-7 (pbk.)
   1. Wood-carving. 2. Wood-carved figurines. 3. Teddy bears in art. I. Title.
TT199.7.S76   1996
731.4'62--dc20   95-36311
                                            CIP

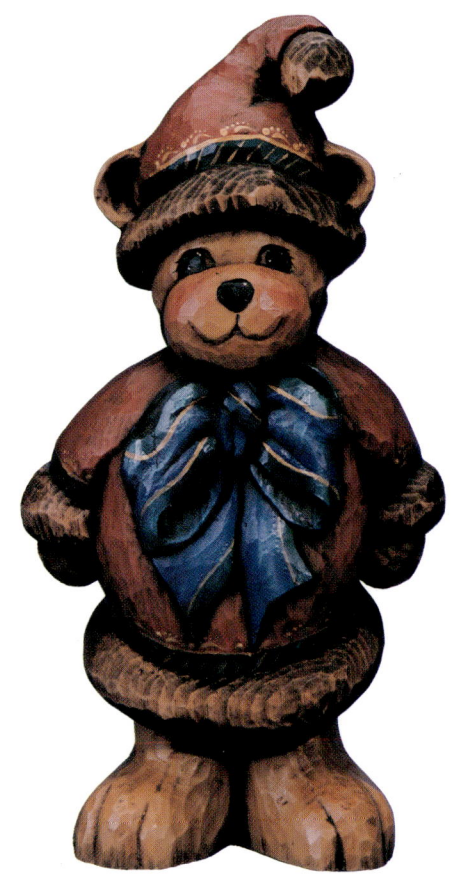

Published by Schiffer Publishing, Ltd.
77 Lower Valley Road
Atglen, PA 19310
Please write for a free catalog.
This book may be purchased from the publisher.
Please include $2.95 postage.
Try your bookstore first.

We are interested in hearing from authors
with book ideas on related subjects.

CONTENTS

INTRODUCTION ———————————————— 4
PROJECT PATTERN ———————————————— 6
CARVING THE TEDDY BEAR ———————————————— 10
PAINTING THE TEDDY BEAR ———————————————— 36
THE GALLERY AND PATTERNS ———————————————— 44

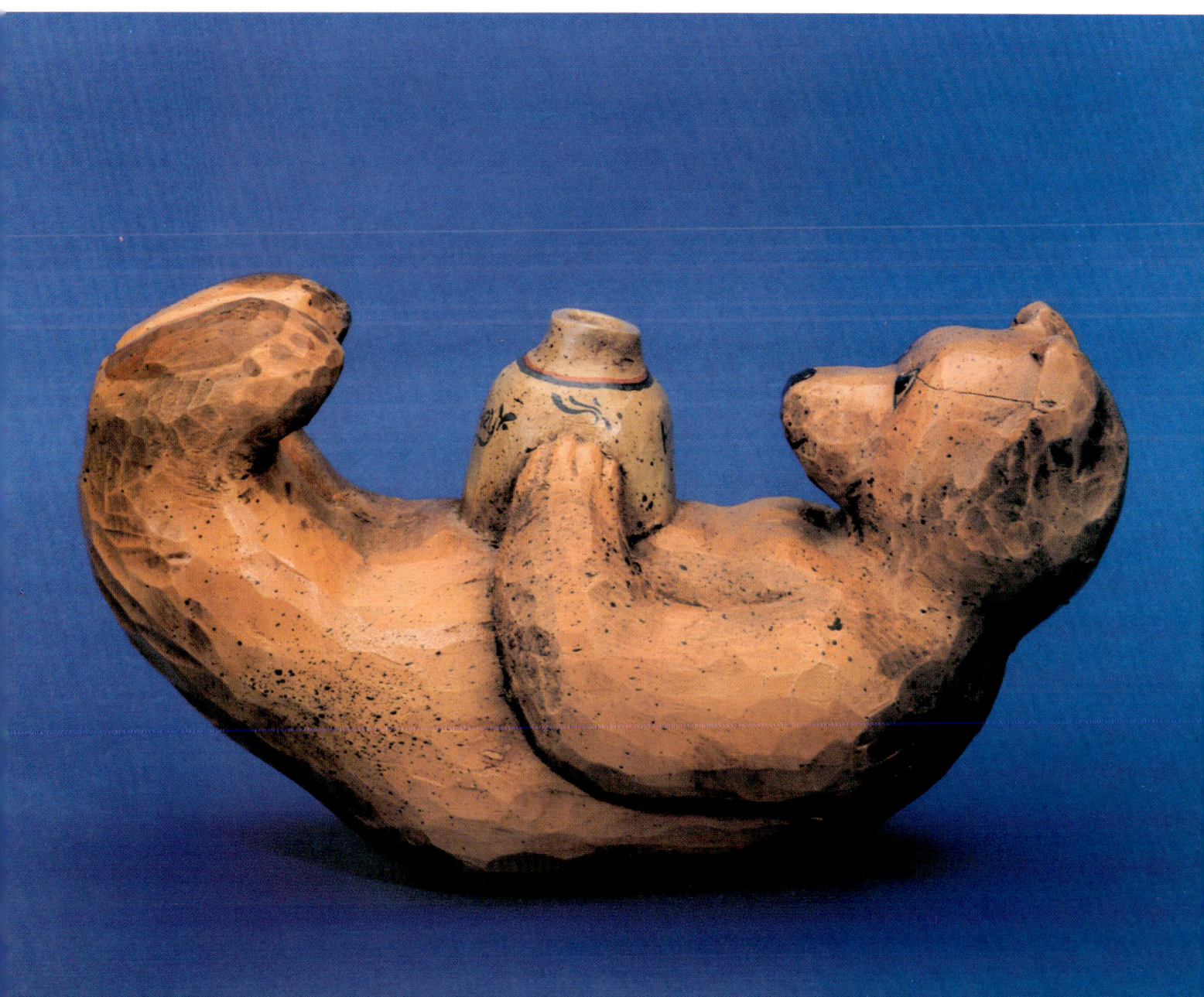

INTRODUCTION

What is it about bears that make them inspire such affection in people? Perhaps it is because they are so rotund, furry and lovable, and always on the prowl for juicy berries, honey or fish. They don't seem to be in any particular hurry and tend to get into trouble because of their overwhelming curiosity.

But if there is a toy store there will be a multitude of bears. If there is a newborn baby there will be a fluffy plush bear and possibly "Teddy Bear" wallpaper and bed clothes. If there is a library there are countless bear characters. The same holds true for children's entertainment. And the fascination with bears goes way beyond children. They have worked their way into the hearts of adults too, so that the chances are good that you know someone who collects bears.

The bears in this book are wonderful little characters that invoke their own stories. I couldn't help but giggle as my blocks of Sugar Pine transformed into "Honey Bear" with his honey pot, "Baby Bear" in diapers, "School Bear," "Santa Bear," "Sleeping Bear" and "Teddy Bear Boy" who should really have a sling shot in his hand.

With all the colored pictures, patterns and step-by-step instructions for both carving and painting, you will find a great deal of pleasure creating your favorite bear. Feel free to inquire about paint color, pre-cut Sugar Pine blanks or any other concerns by writing or calling:

Kelley S. Stadelman
P.O. Box 191
North Plains, Oregon 97133
(503) 647-0892

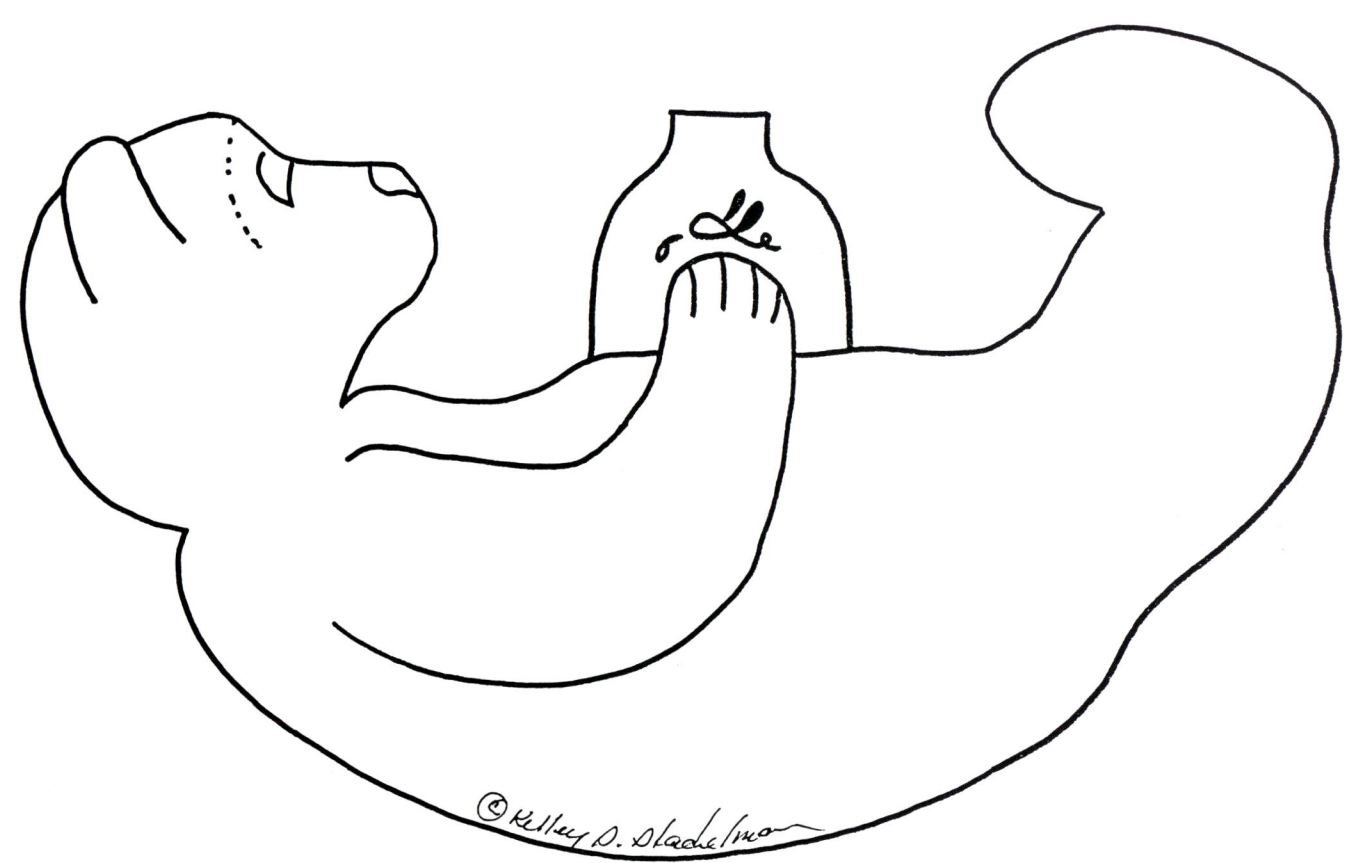

—Carving Tools and Terms

Chisel: A tool with a flat cutting edge. It may have a single or double bevel.

Skew Chisel: This chisel has a double bevel and is slanted obliquely along the chisel edge.

Gouge: A tool with a single bevel and a cutting edge that is curved or shaped in a compound configuration.

Bench Knife: A carving tool with the cutting edge parallel to the handle.

Disposable blades: These blades fit into a special handle. They are made of thin metal and are extremely sharp. Generally they are not resharpened.

—Care of Tools

After investing in quality tools, care should be taken to maintain their sharpness. Contact between your tools and surfaces other than wood may chip and dull them. Most towns have fine cutlery stores which provide sharpening services. However, I am of the opinion that the art of sharpening should be learned by every carver. There are several books that will give you instructions in the techniques of sharpening.

—Carving Safety

Remember, you are using a sharp tool. You may become comfortable with carving tools in your hand, but they are obviously more dangerous than a pen or a paint brush. I have held a paint brush in my mouth, scratched my head with one, and even used on as a pointer. Doing these common gestures with a carving tool could cause harm to you or someone else. Protect yourself and your carving companions. Avoid pointing or talking with your hands with a carving tool in hand. Avoid placing tools on the table top so that they might roll off the table and onto (or into) someone's foot.

Whenever possible carve on the table top, not in your lap. Build up your chair with a pillow or two so you are well above your carving. Place your wood in a clamp or on some type of device to hold it in place. I like to use the non-skid grid that is used under throw rugs.

I have cut myself. I do not cut myself often anymore. I have a good sense for what my tools and wood will do. Carving when you are tired or tense will increase the chance of being cut. Take many little breaks. Know your limits. Be careful and have a good time!

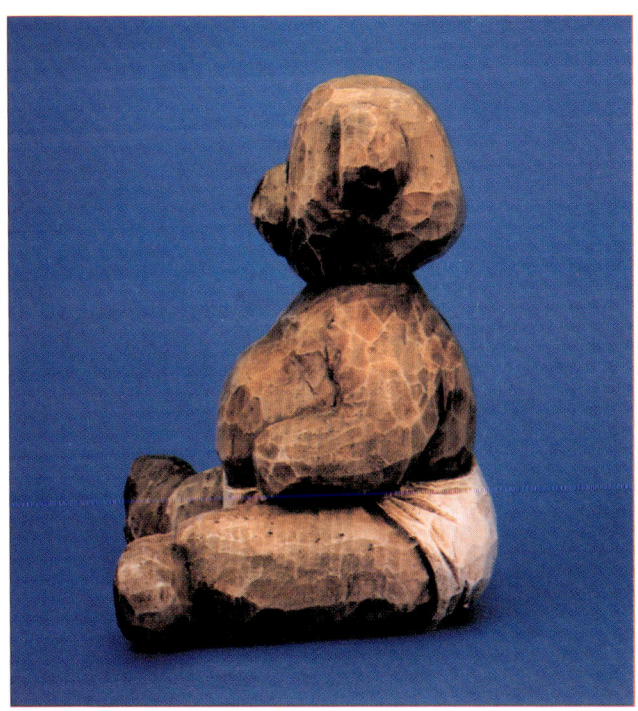

THE PROJECT PATTERN

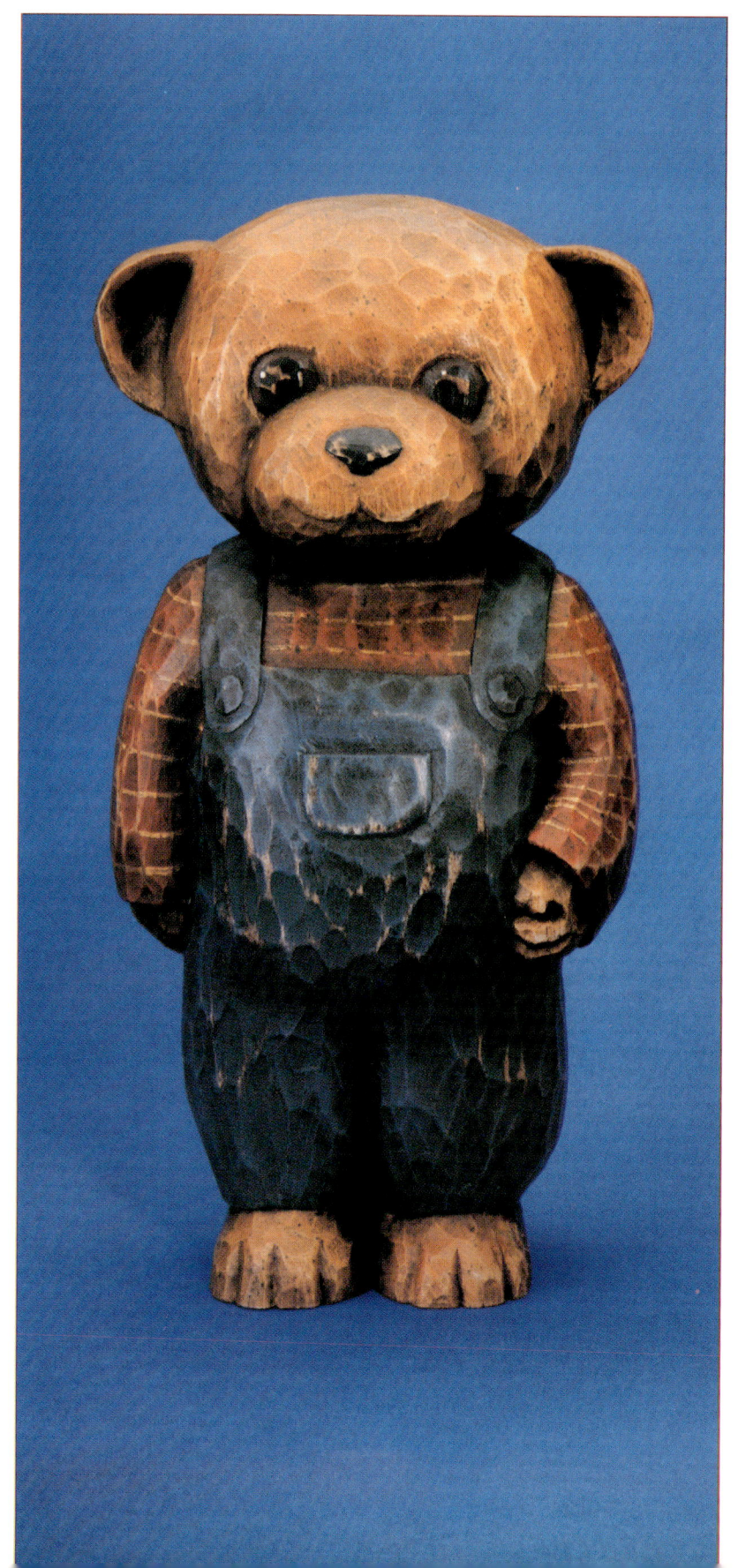

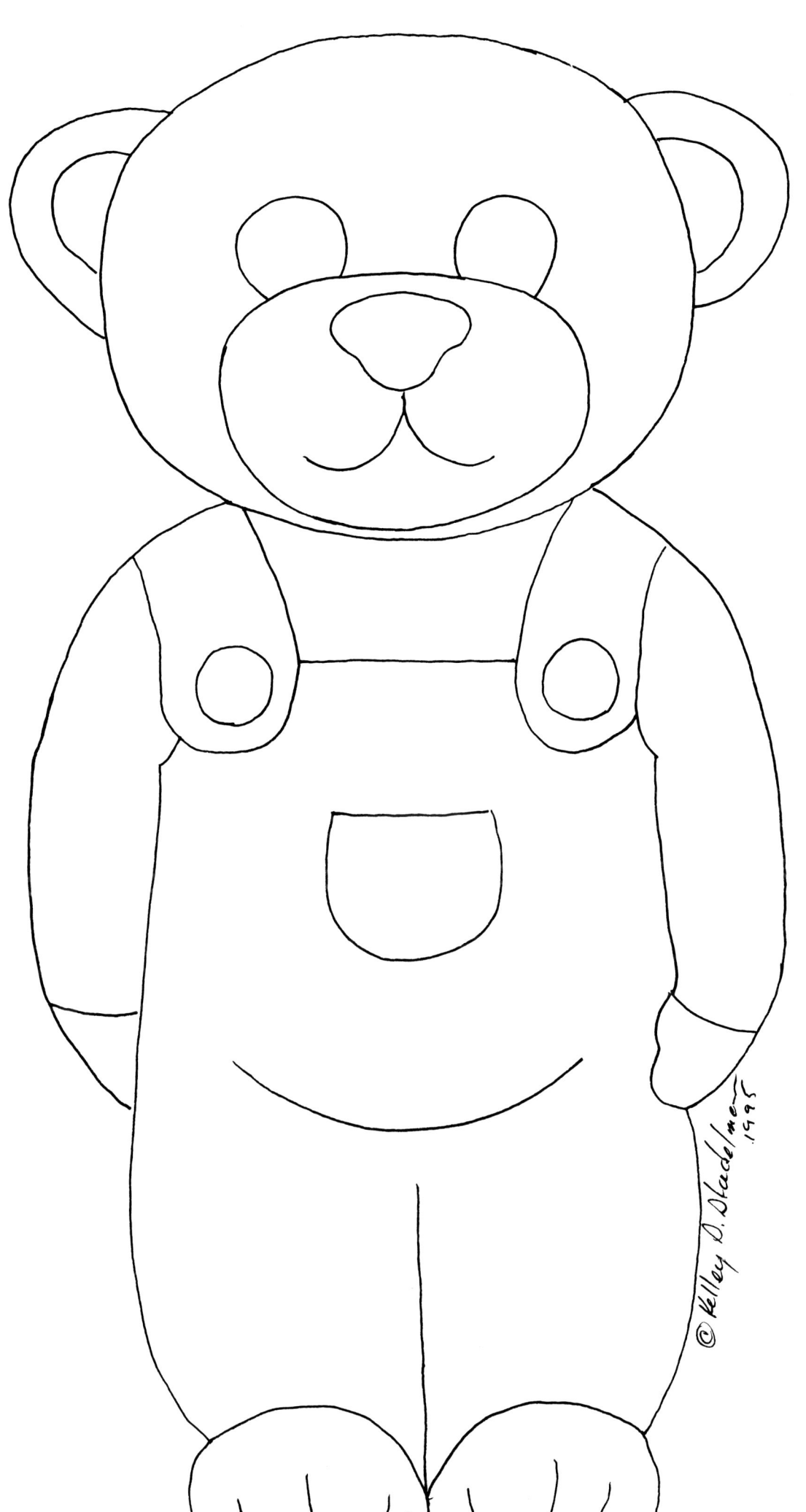

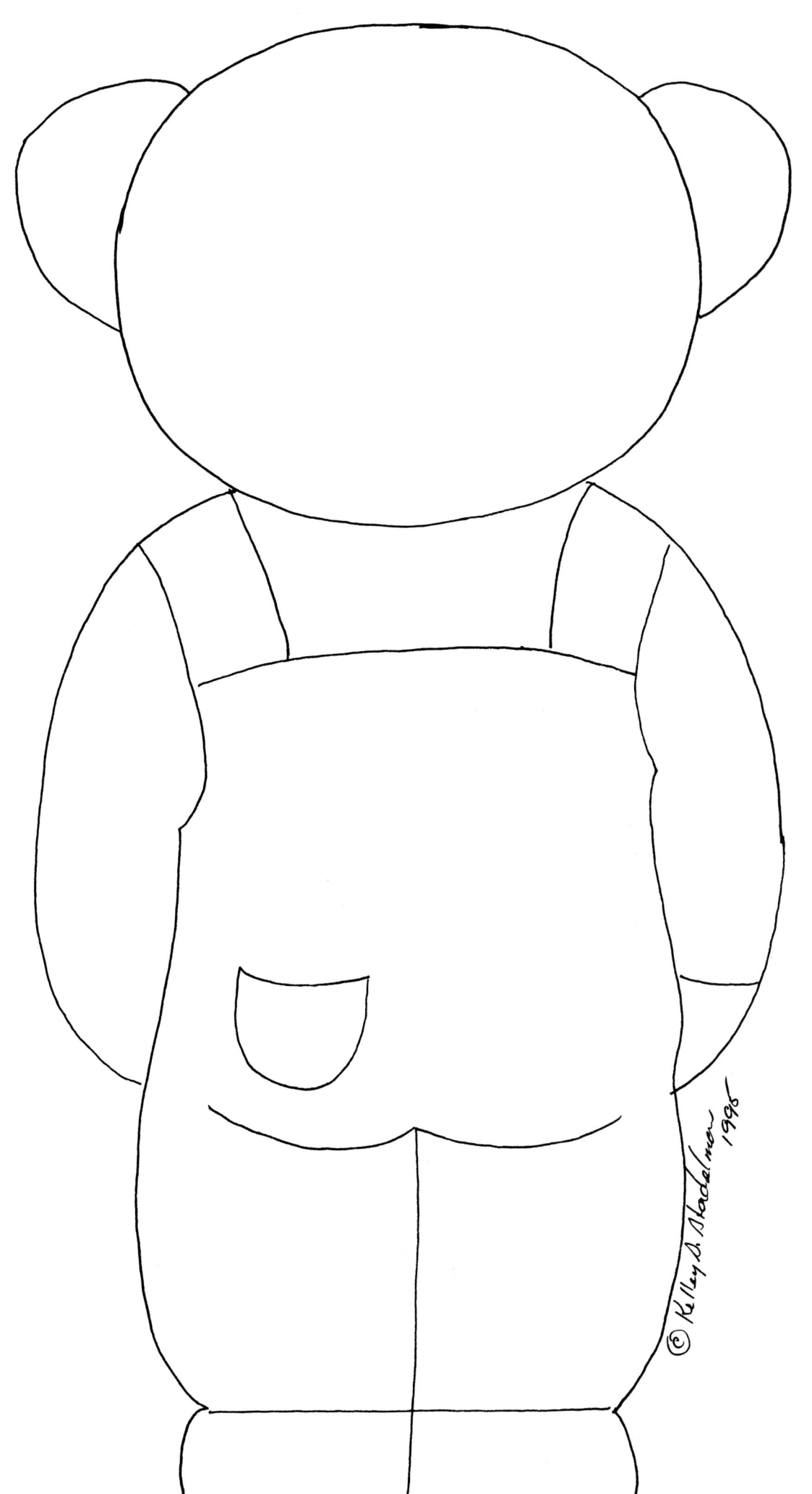

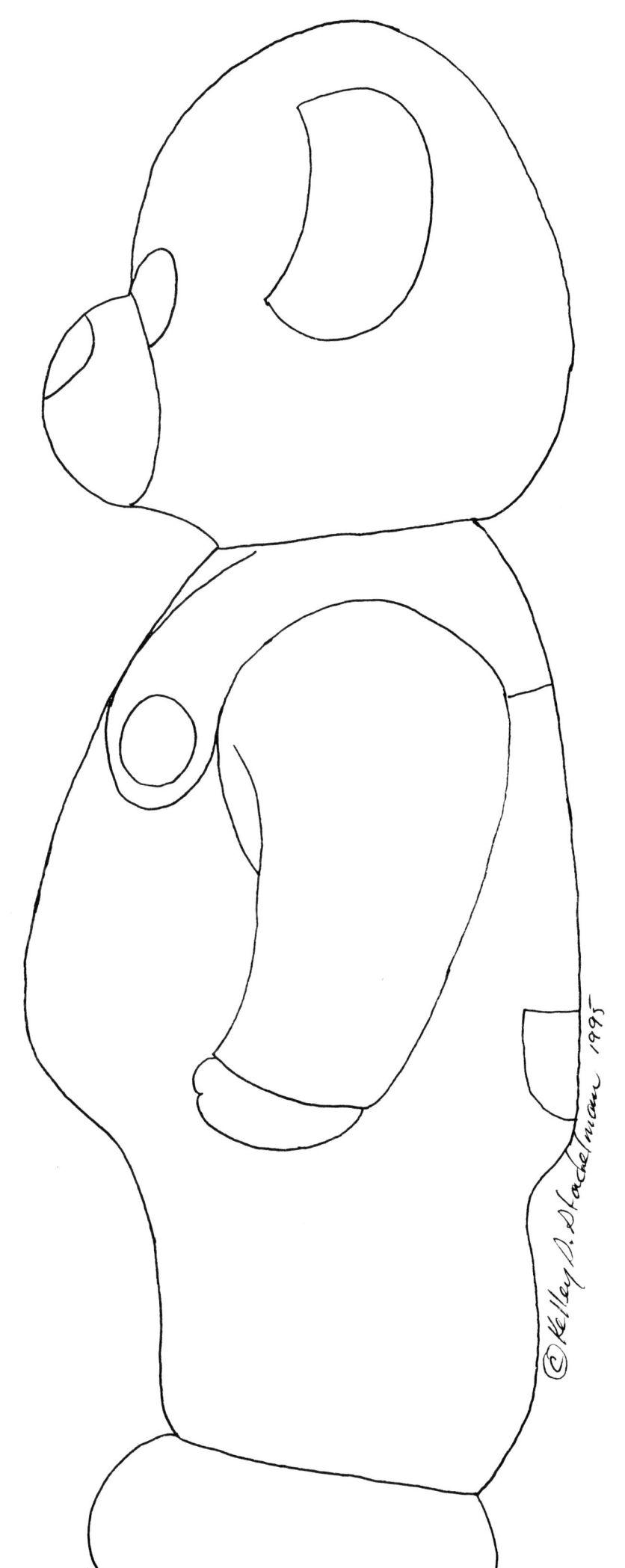

CARVING THE TEDDY BEAR

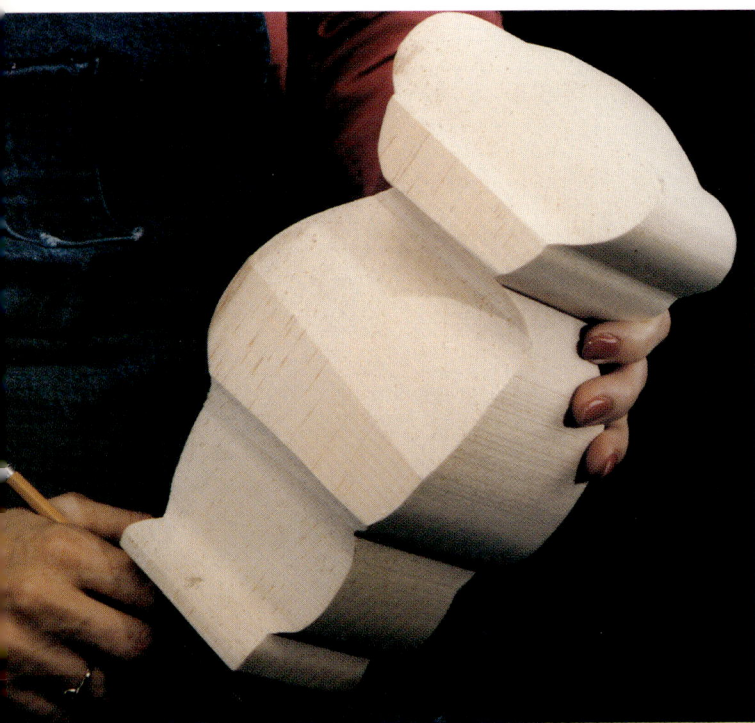

Cut the blank from 4 inch stock. This is sugar pine, but other woods could be used as well.

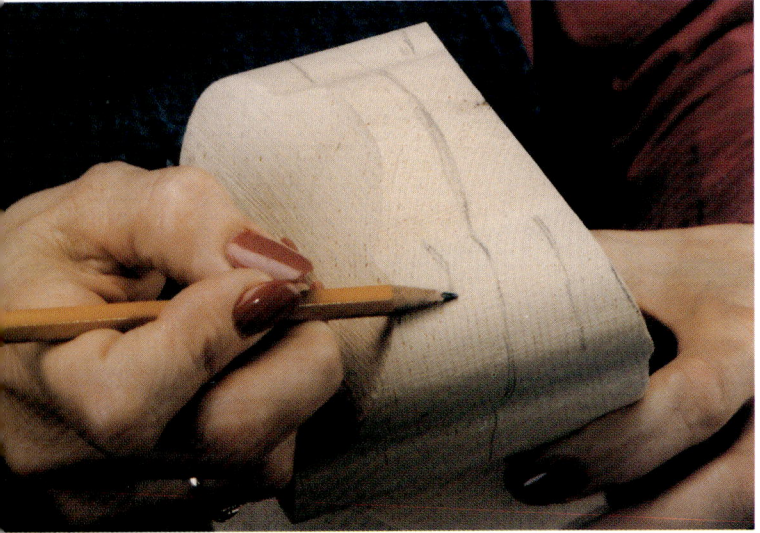

Draw a center line over the top of the head and mark the thickness of the ears.

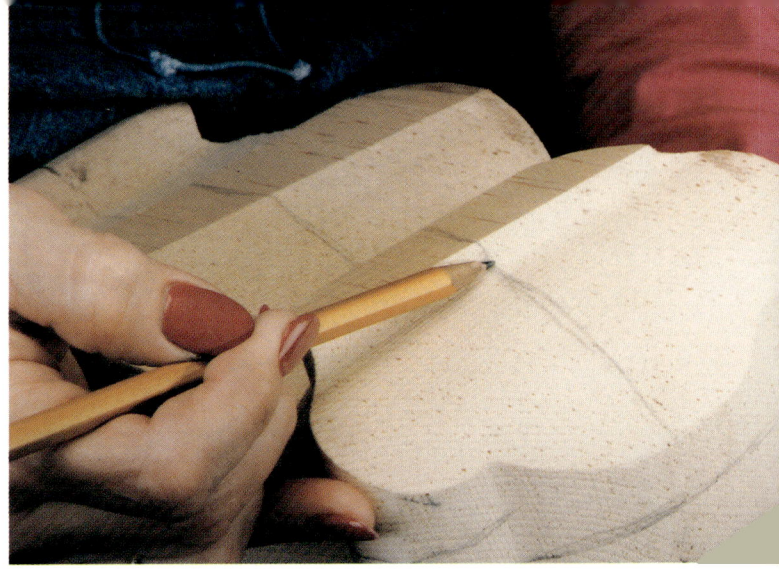

Draw another center line down the front...

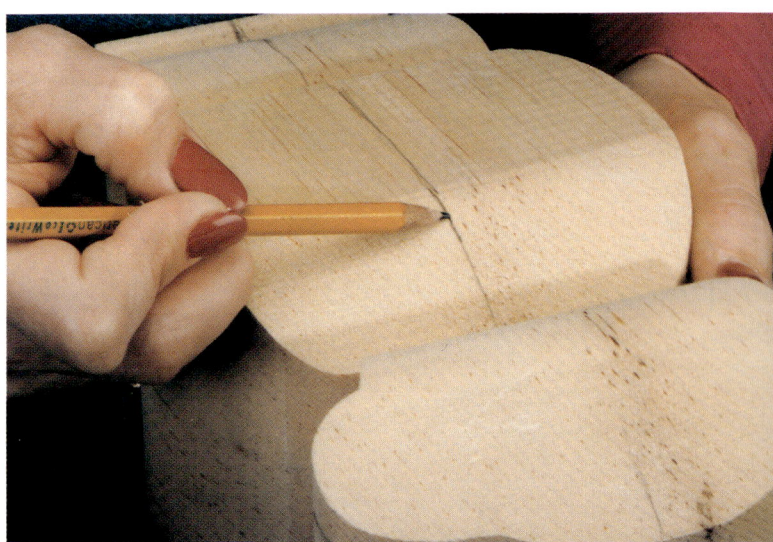

and back.

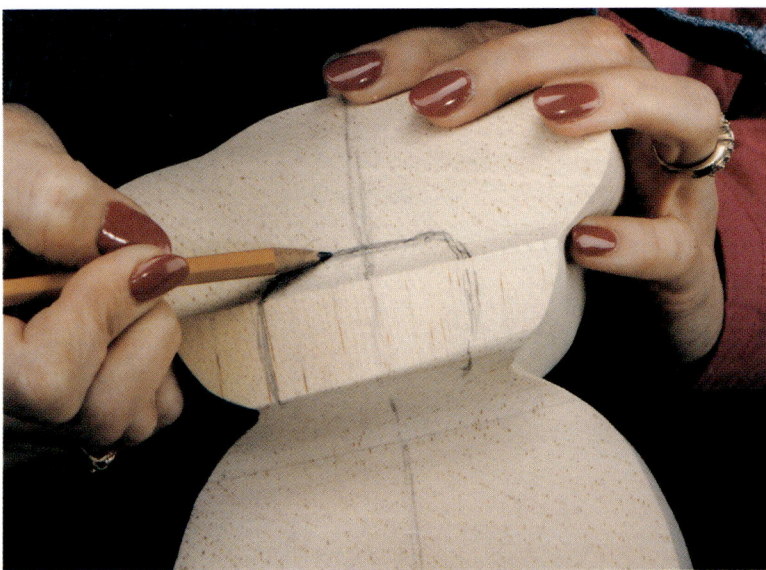

Referring to the pattern, draw in the rough shape of the muzzle.

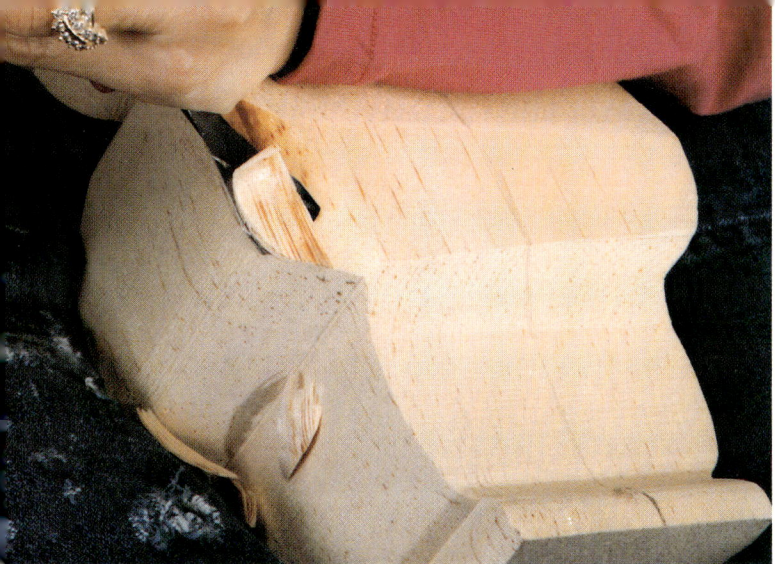

Knock off the corners all around.

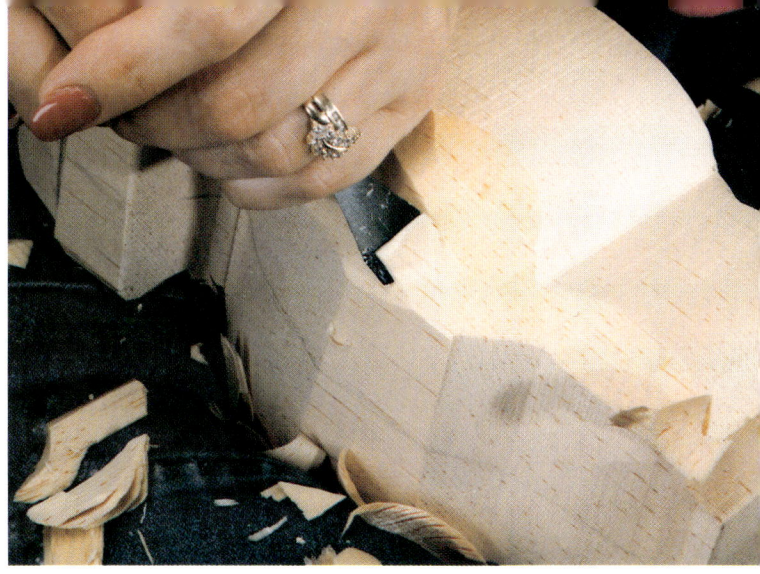

You want to take quite a bit off the corner. If you take off too little, the figure looks square and unnatural.

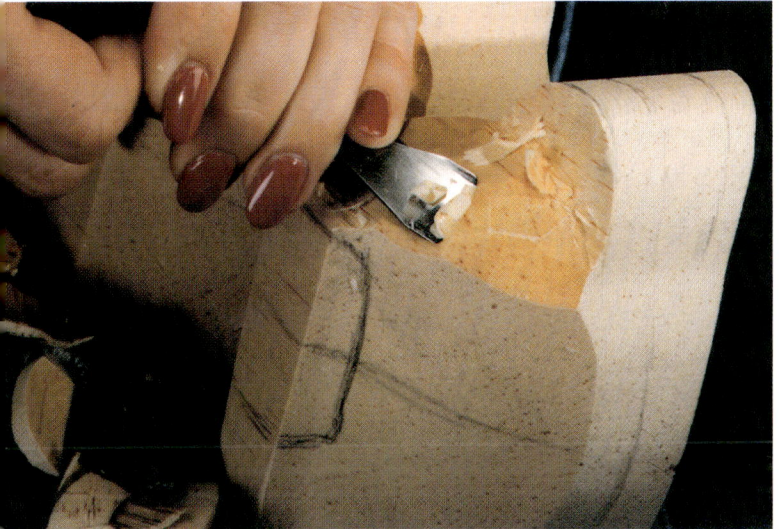

At the head, trim the front the ear straight in and knock off the corner of the face.

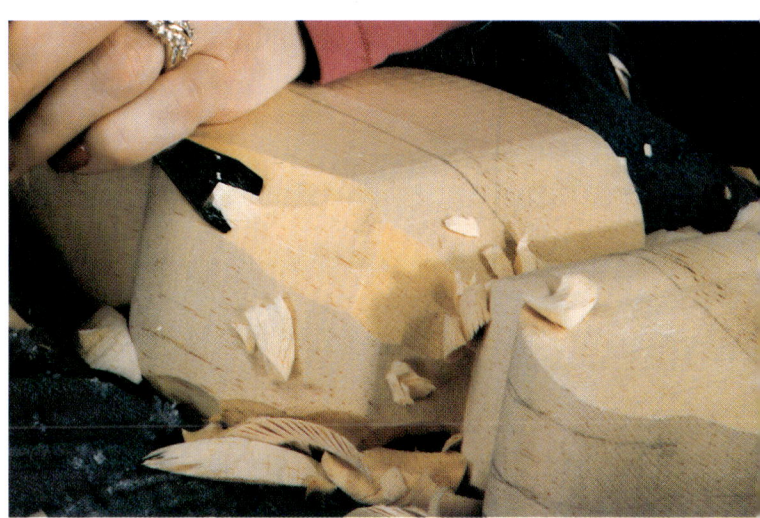

Continue on the back.

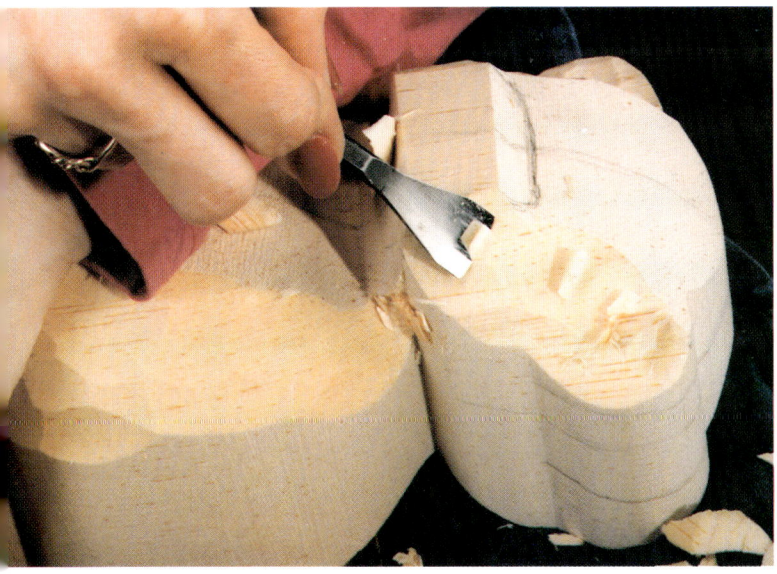

On the face, leave the muzzle intact for now.

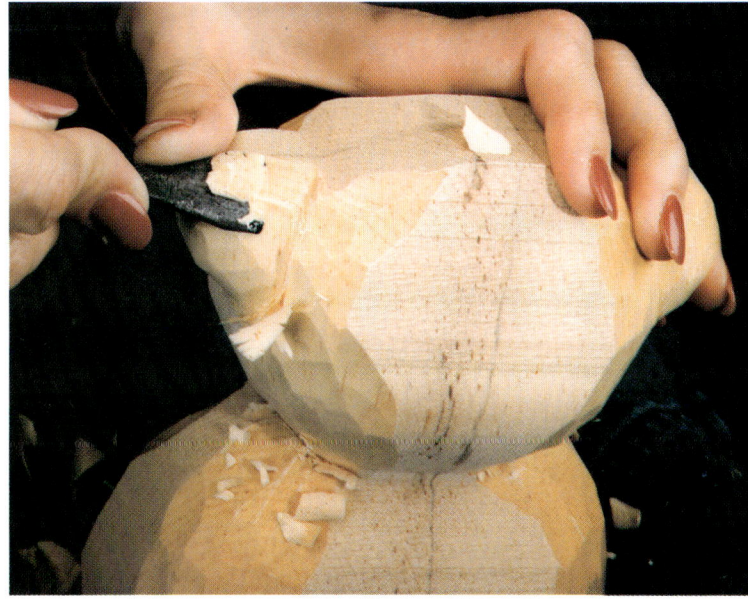

Round the back of the ears.

Round the head down to the center line.

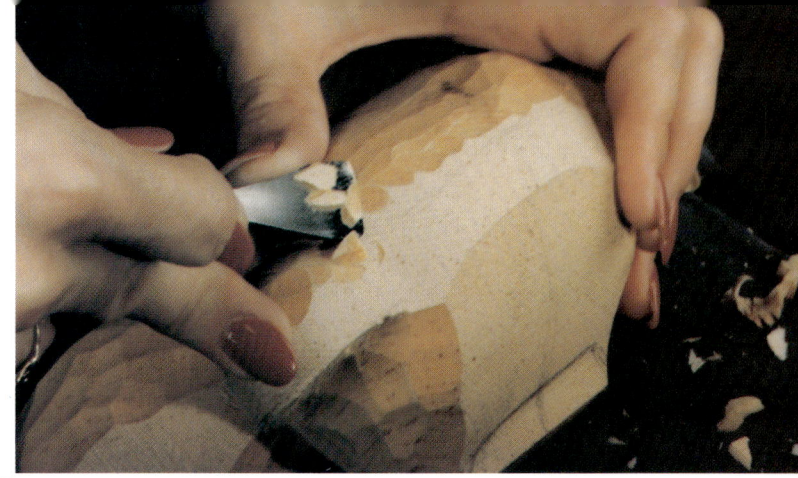

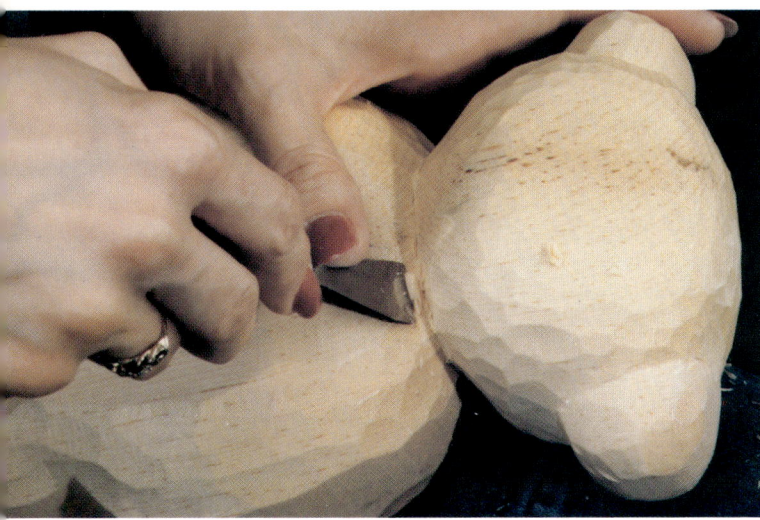

Work from the shoulder and the head to define the neck line.

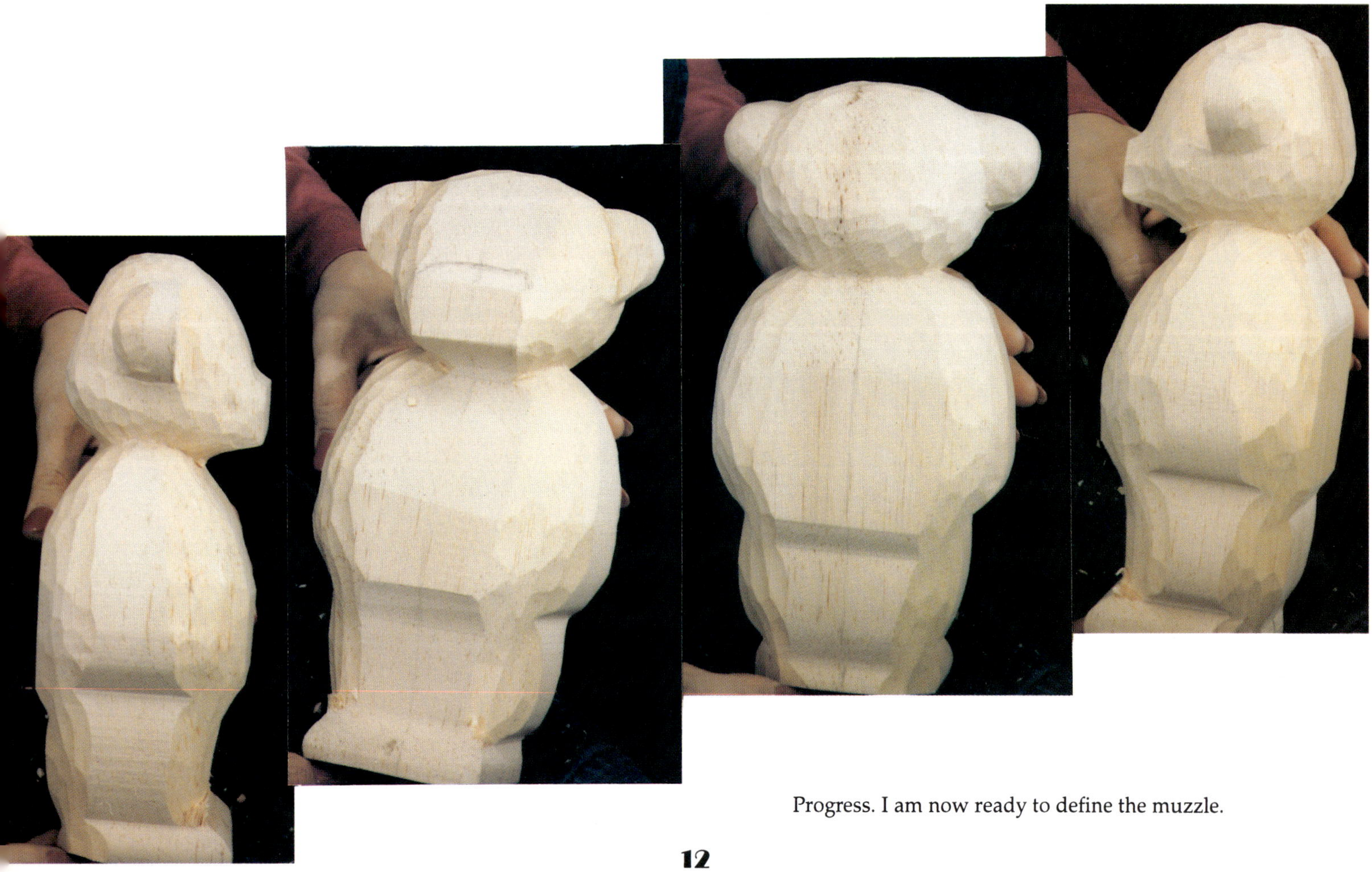

Progress. I am now ready to define the muzzle.

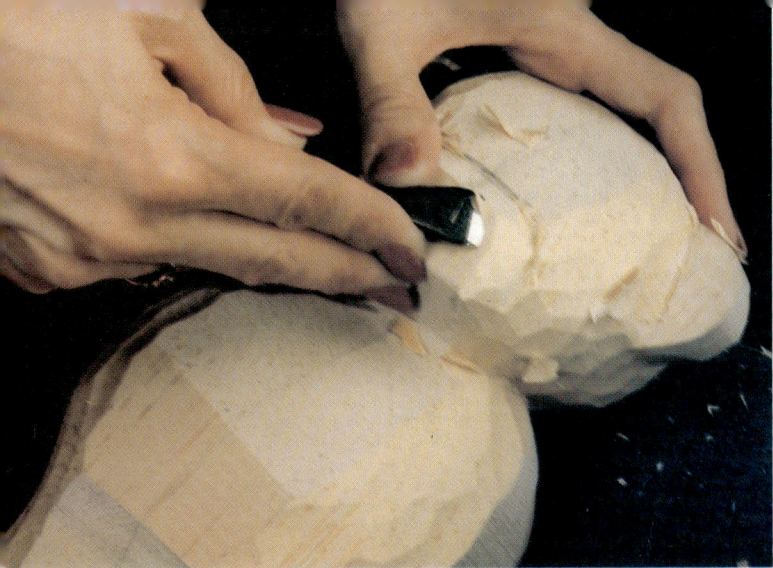

Begin work on the muzzle by knocking off the edges to set the general shape.

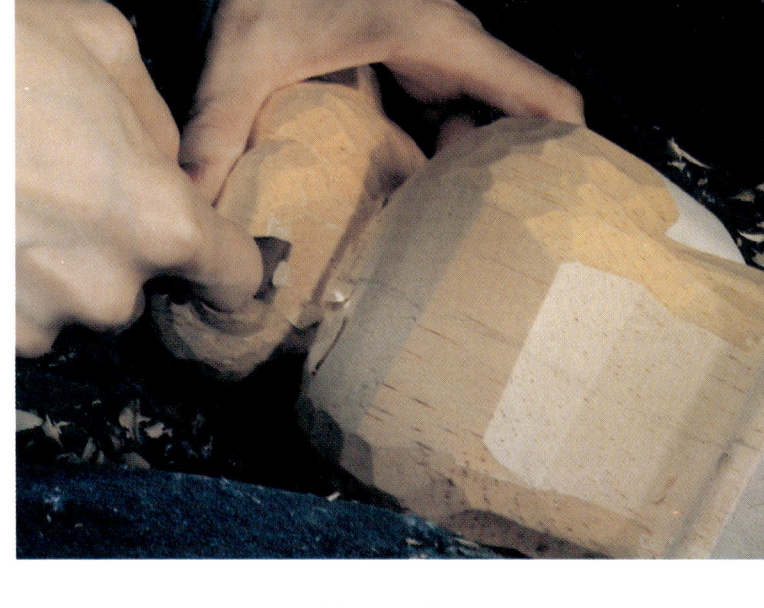

Continue on the underside of the muzzle.

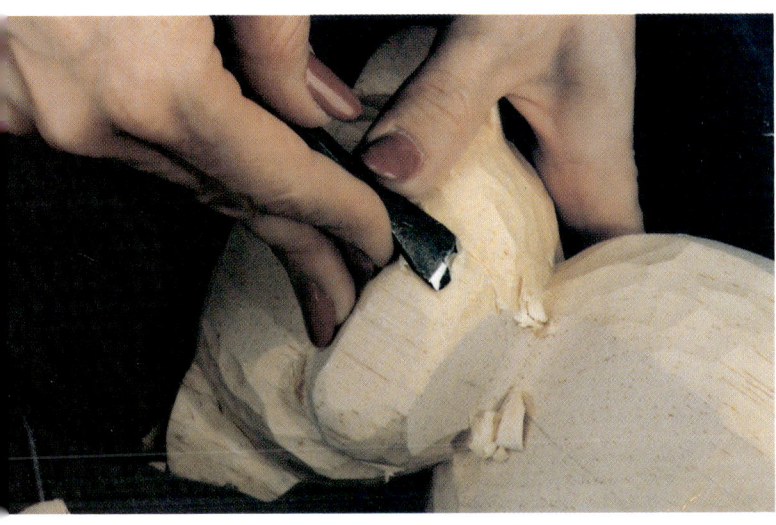

Shaping the side where the muzzle meets the face can be done by holding the gouge cup against the wood.

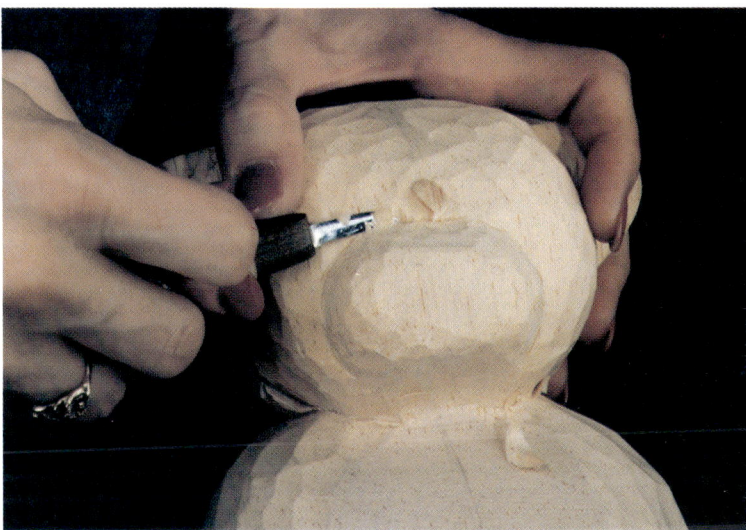

Use the knife to get a nice even border around the muzzle.

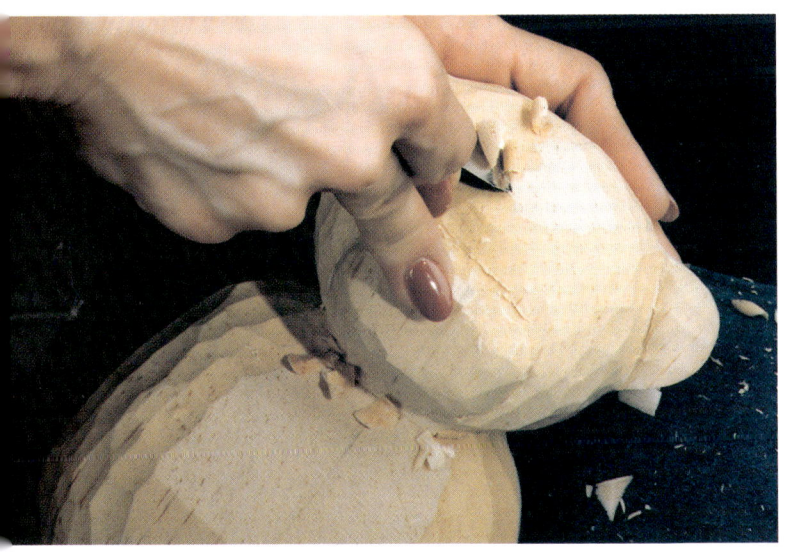

You will need to work on the head and face at the same time to keep things in balance.

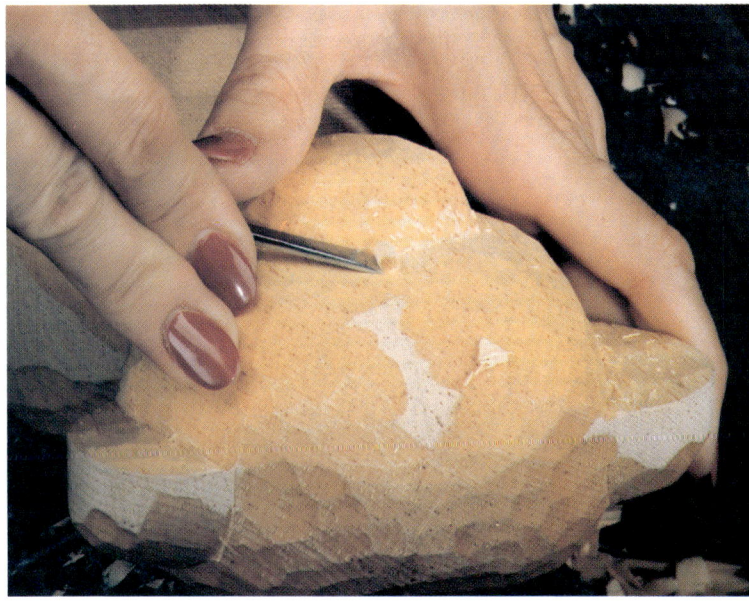

Clean up the carving with a straight chisel.

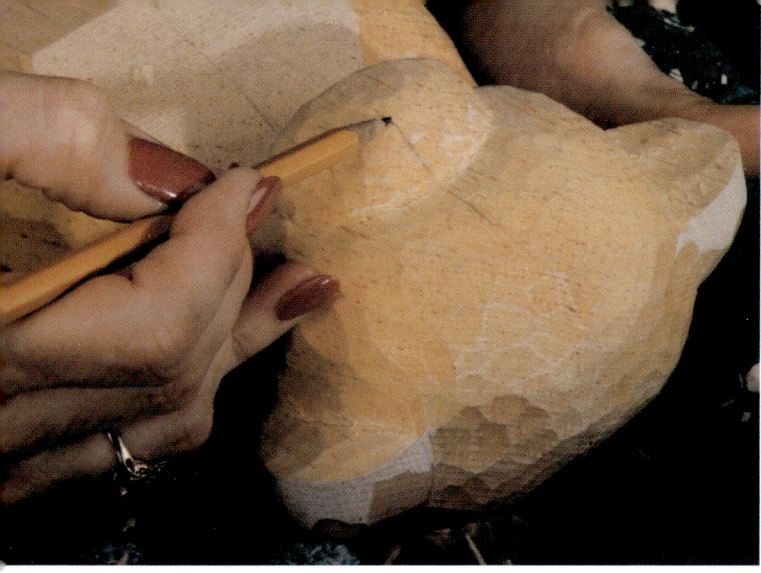

Draw a center line on the face.

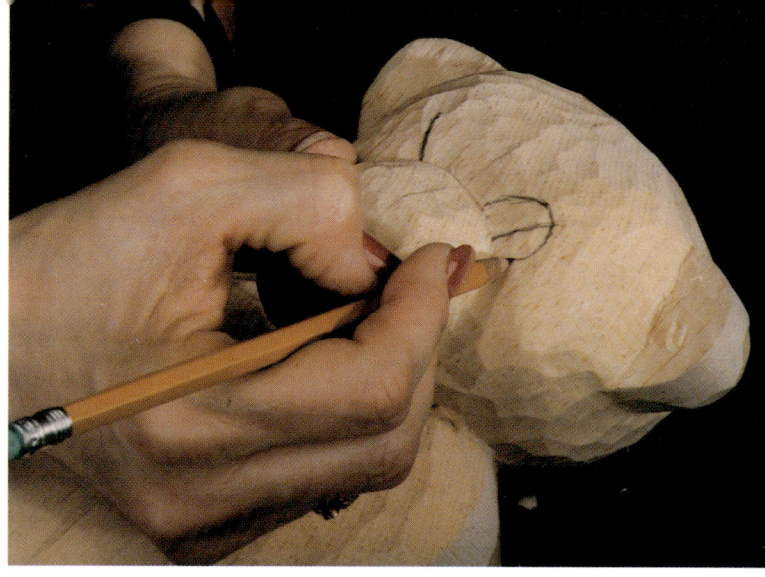

With that line as a center draw an eye that starts and ends at the muzzle.

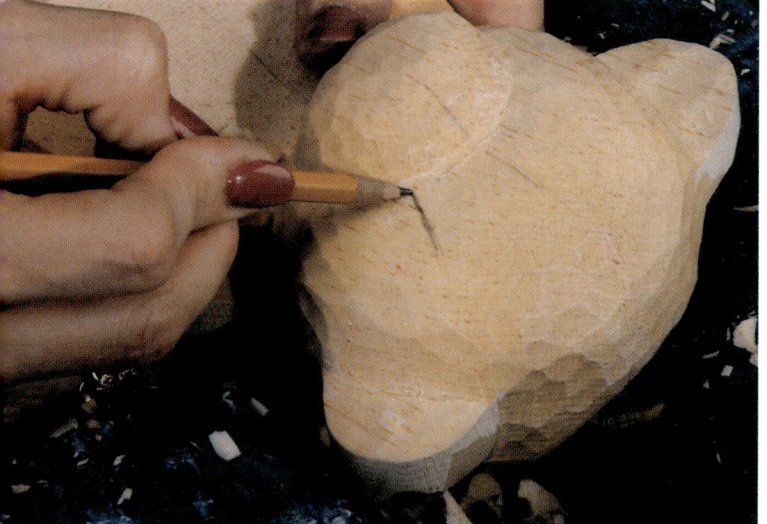

The placement of the eye can be set by drawing a line from the inside of the ear to the muzzle.

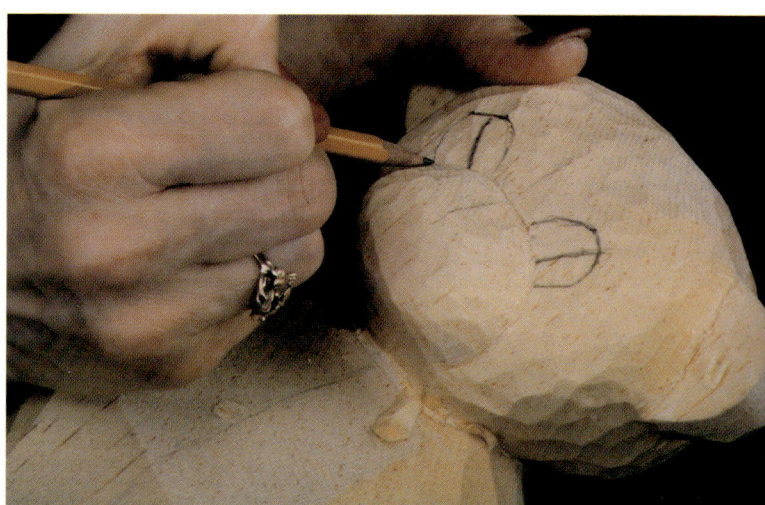

Do the same on the other side.

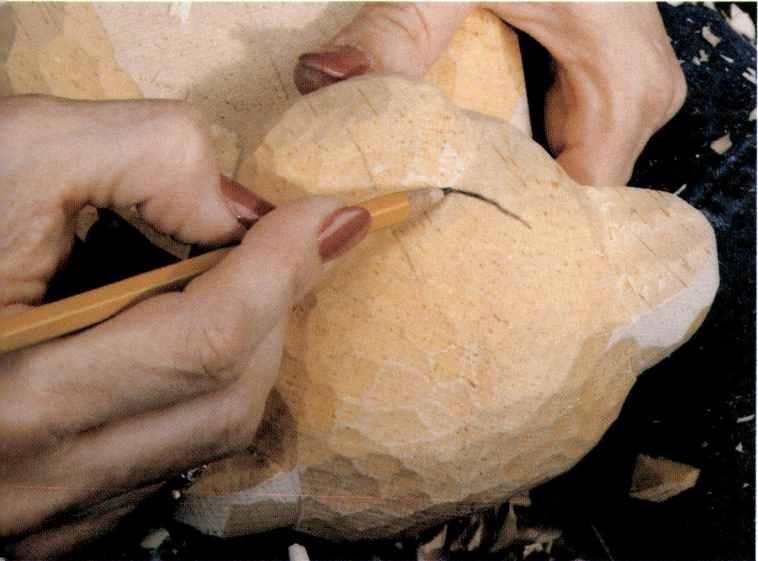

Do the same on the other side.

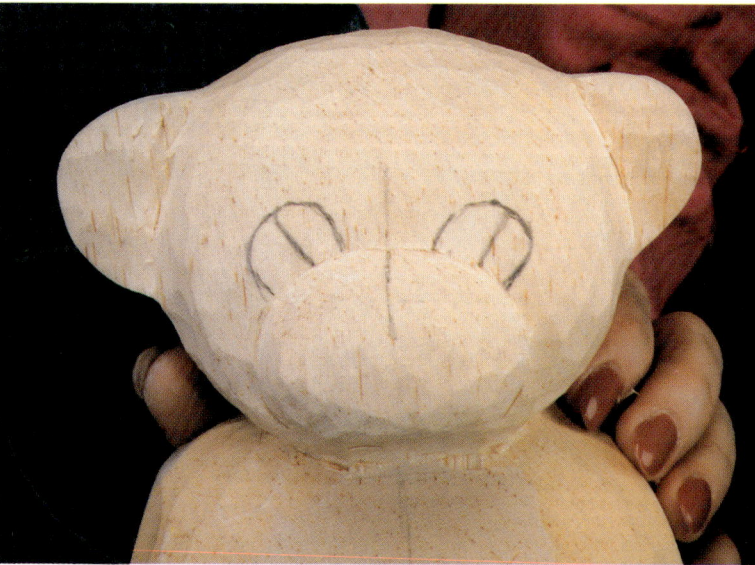

The result. At this point it is easy to see if the face is symmetrical and where corrections need to be made.

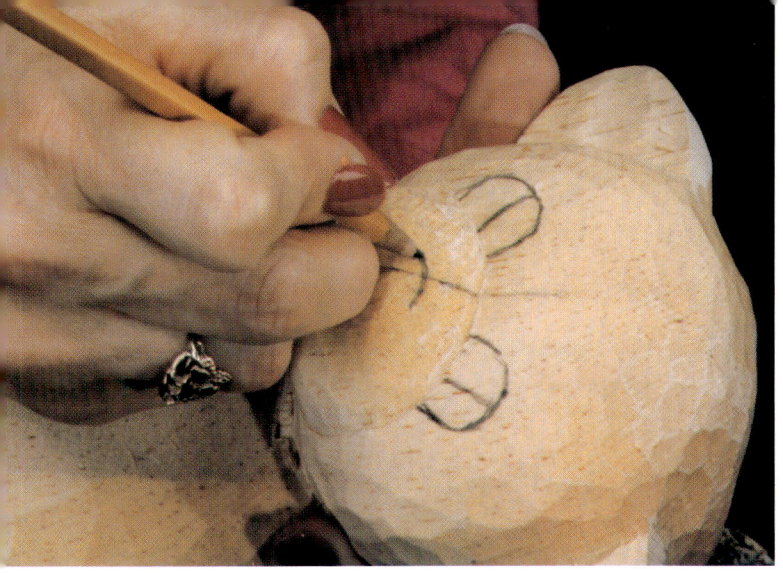

Draw an arch for the top of the nose...

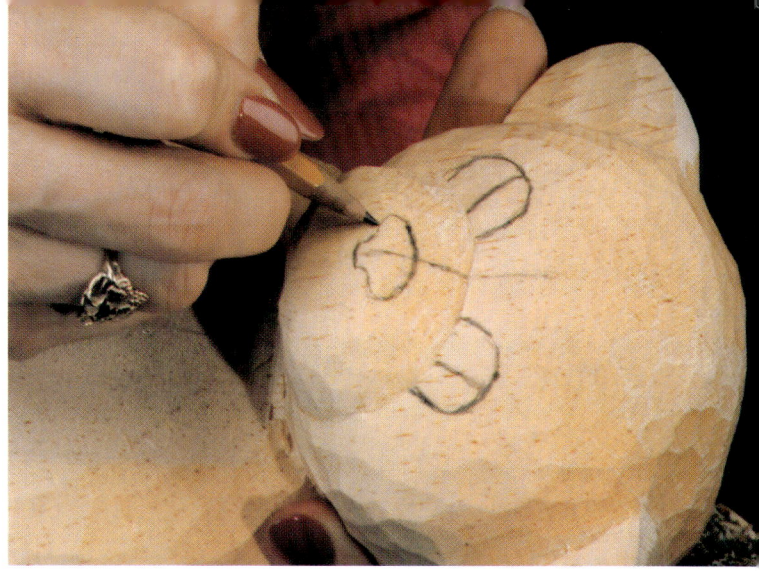

Connect the tops of the nostrils with the top of the nose.

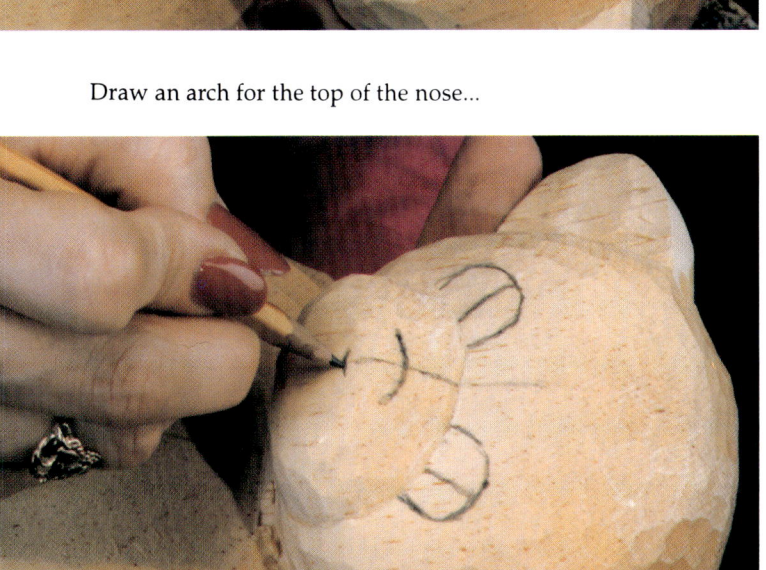

and a smaller arch at the bottom.

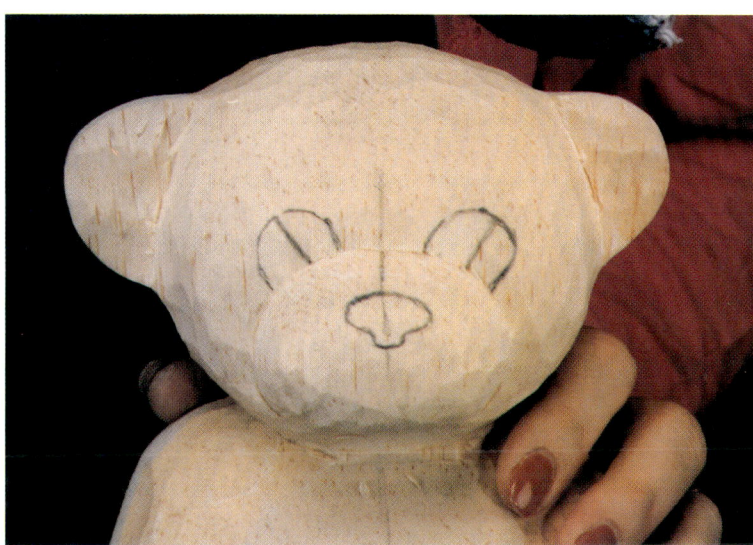

The nose drawn.

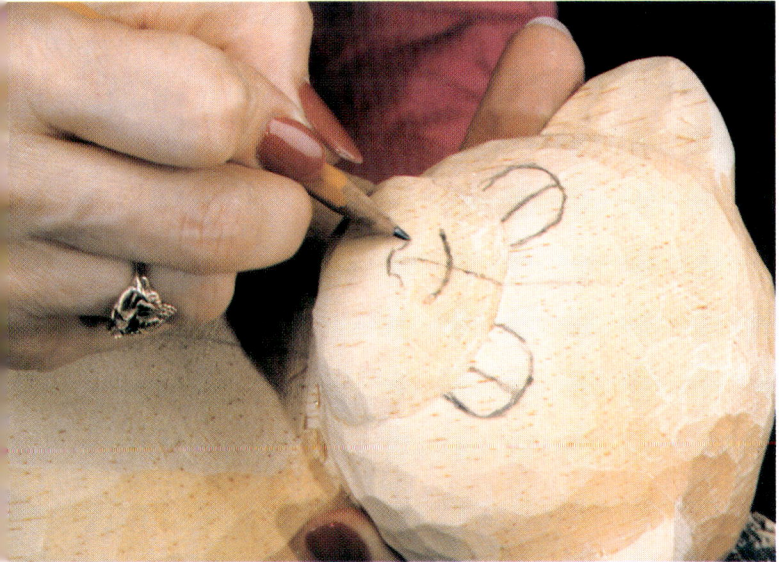

At each side of the bottom arch draw a small inverted arch for the nostrils.

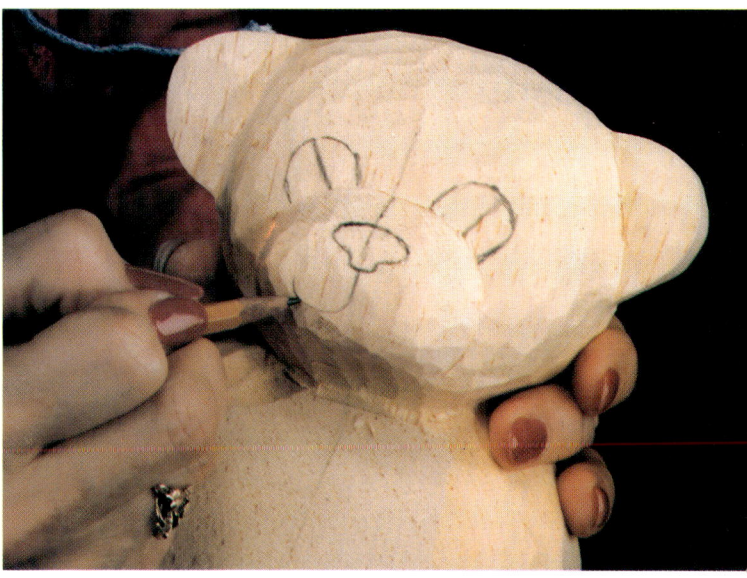

Draw a straight line down from the nose ending in a turned up smile.

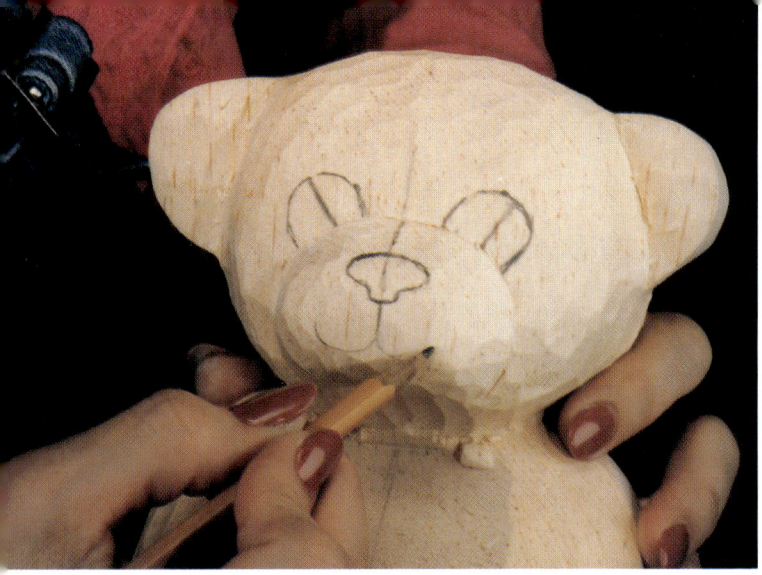

Draw the other side of the smile.

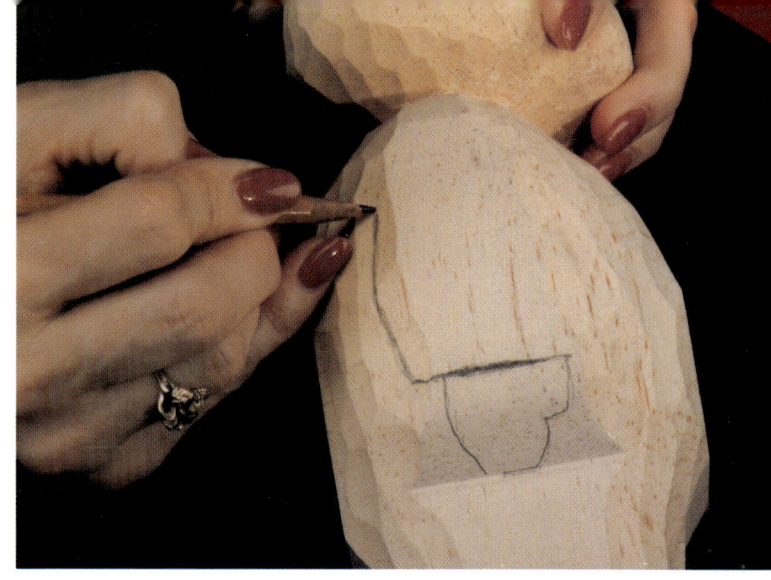

the back of the sleeve...

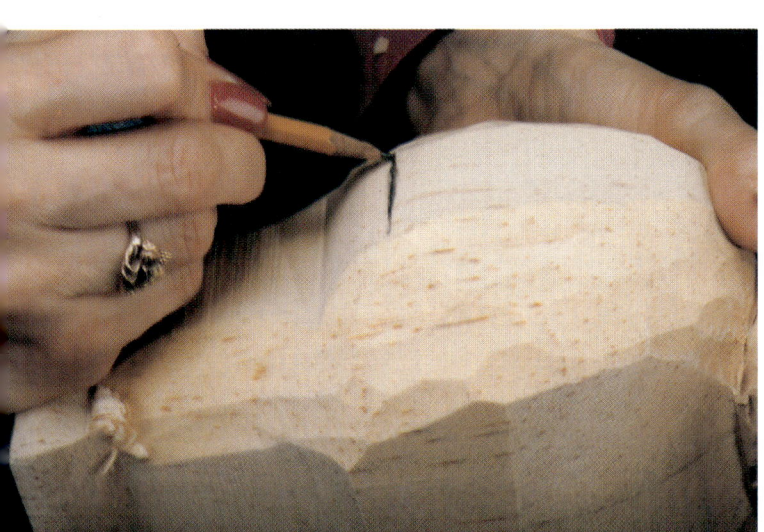

Draw the line of the cuff...

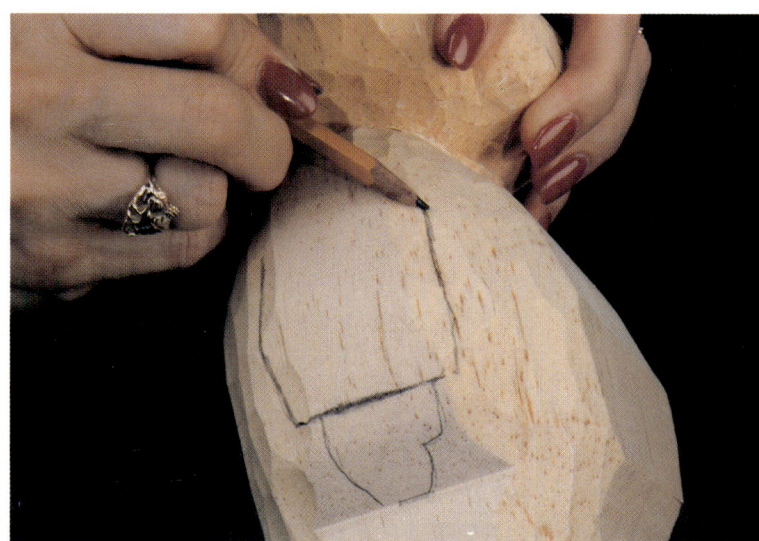

and the front of the sleeve.

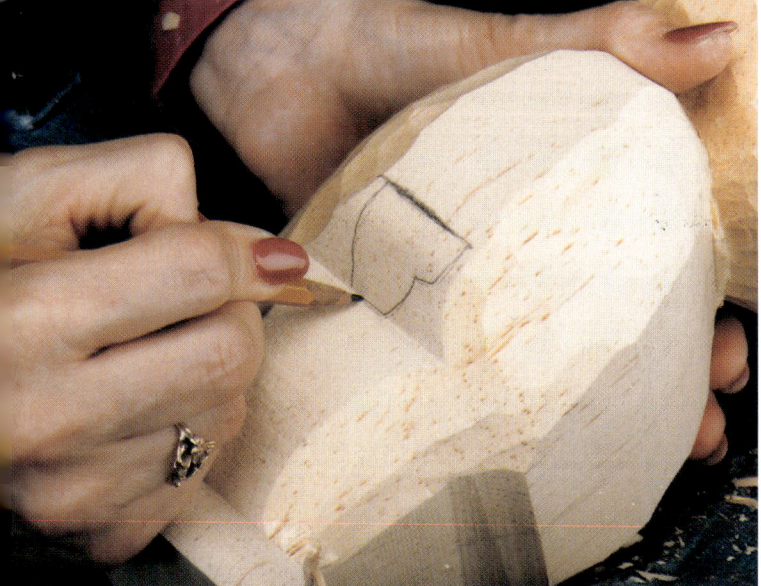

the paw...

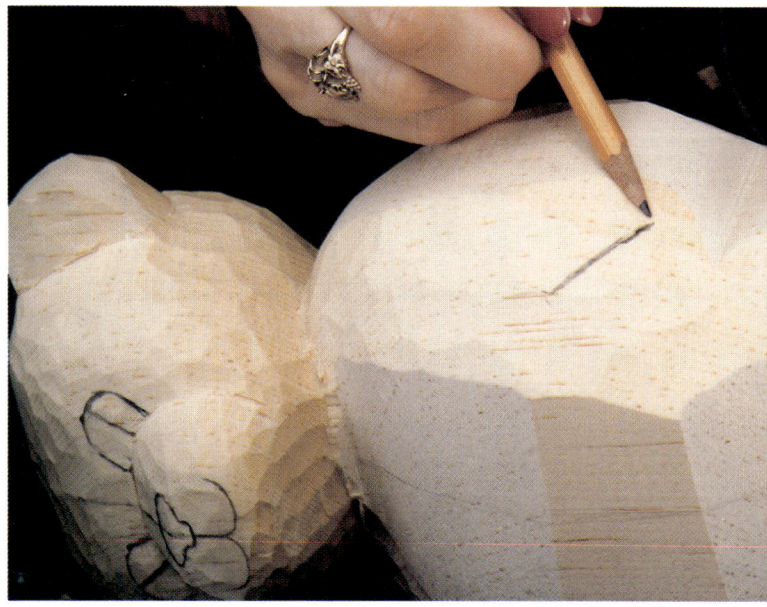

The left arm is bent forward. Draw the cuff at a diagonal.

16

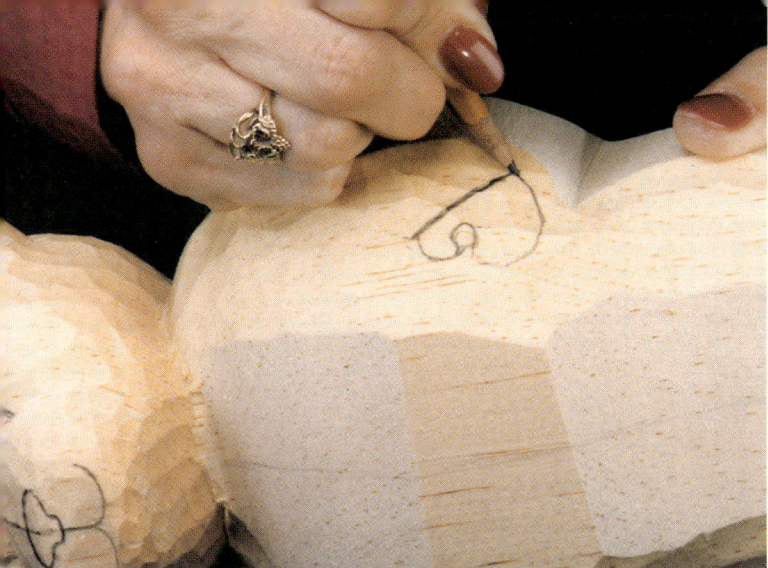

Make a circle for the space in front of the thumb and draw the hand around it.

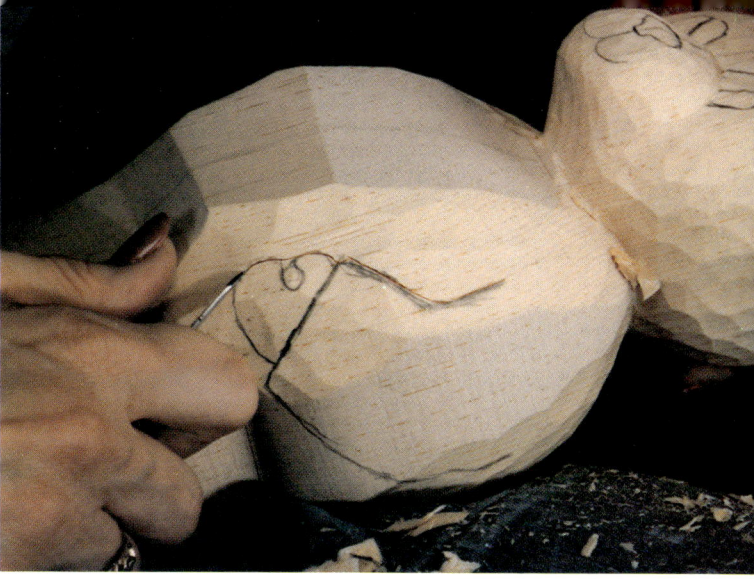

and of the hand.

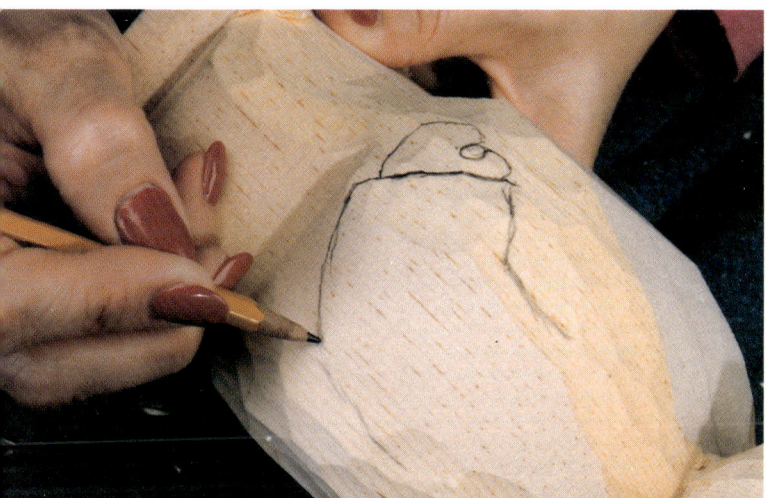

Draw the front and back of the sleeve.

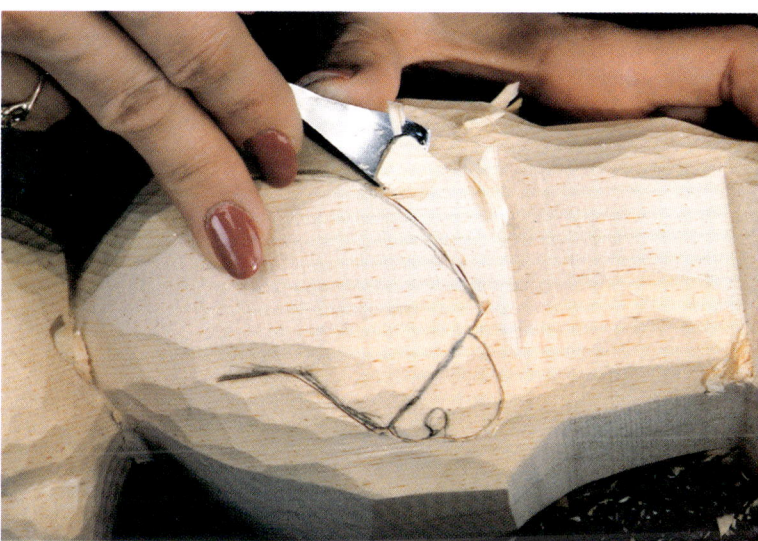

Relieve the wood around the arm and hand with a slicing cut.

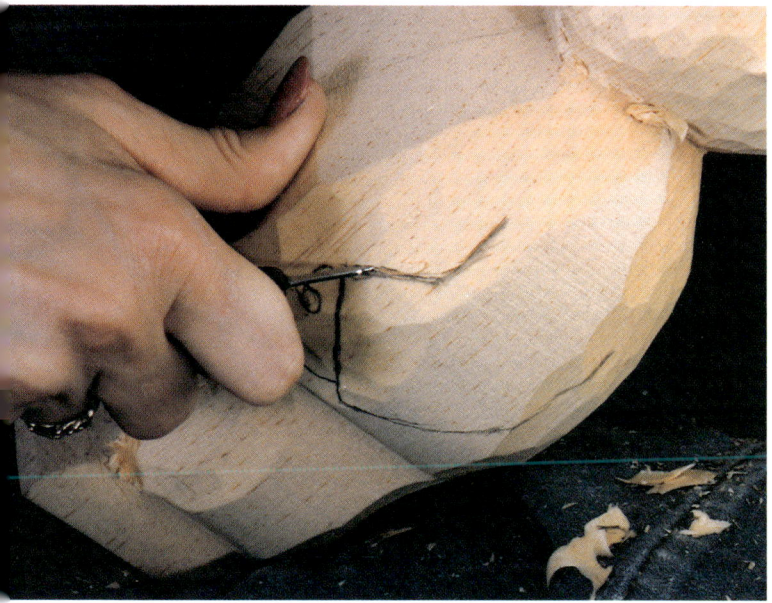

Score straight in along the line of the sleeve...

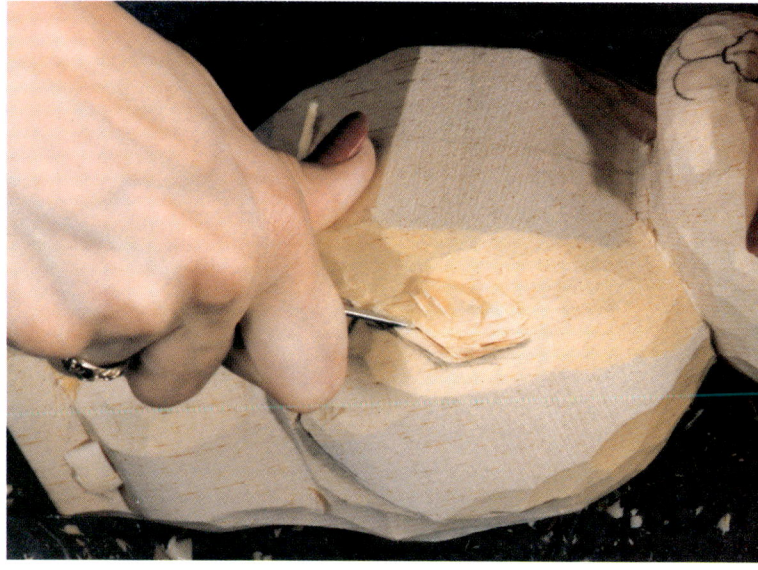

Clean up the cuts and deepen the score line with a knife.

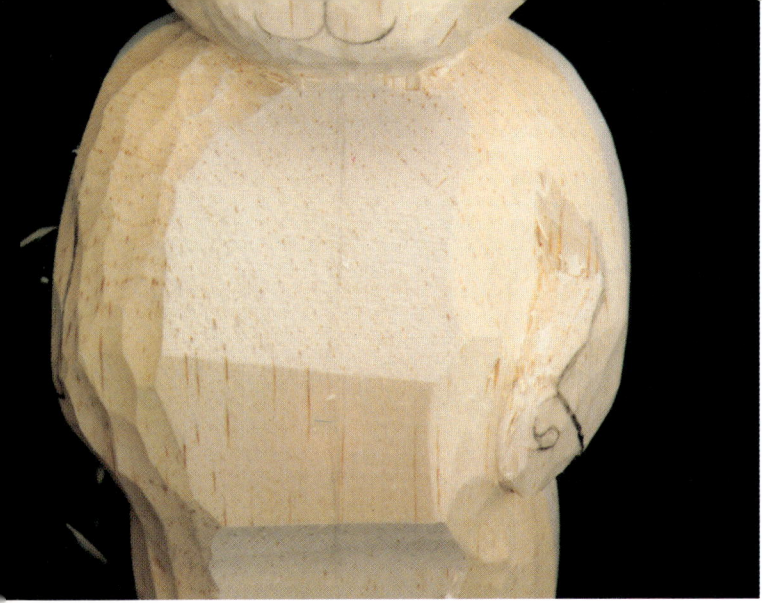

Continue to score and clean until you get to about this depth in the front...

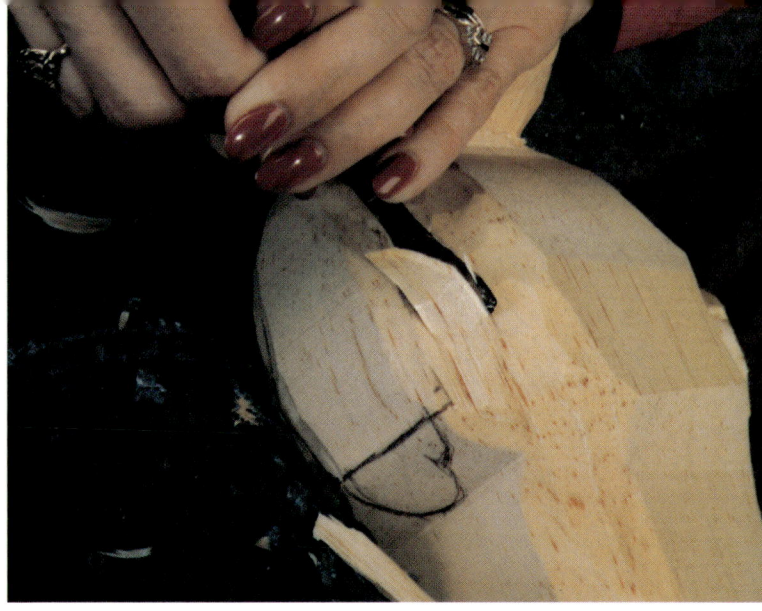

Slice beside the score mark to bring out the arm.

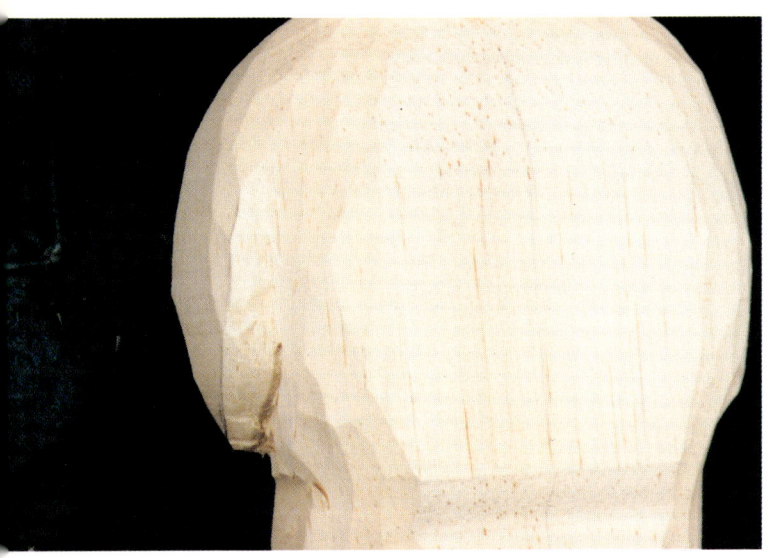

and this in the back. You want the arm to stand out from the body.

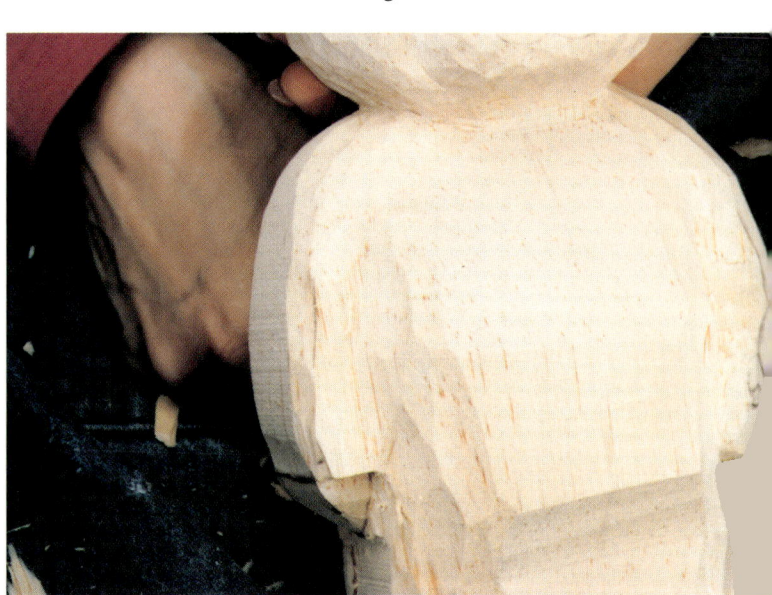

Continue until you get to about this point.

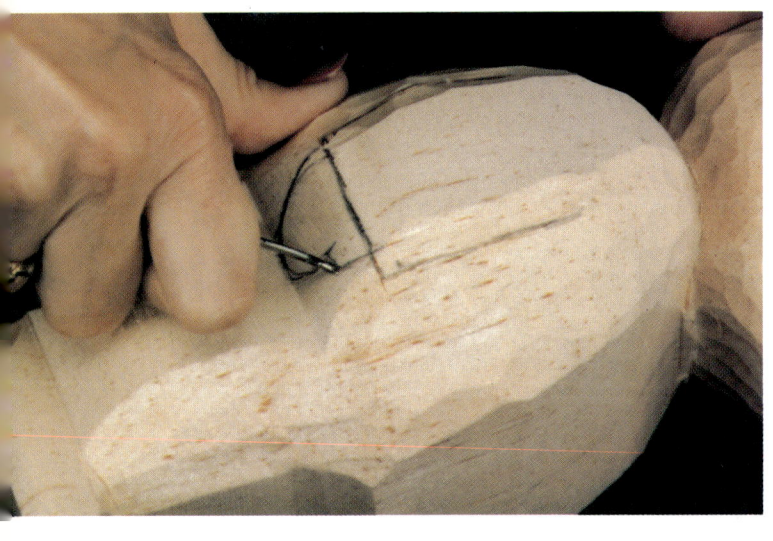

Score around the other arm.

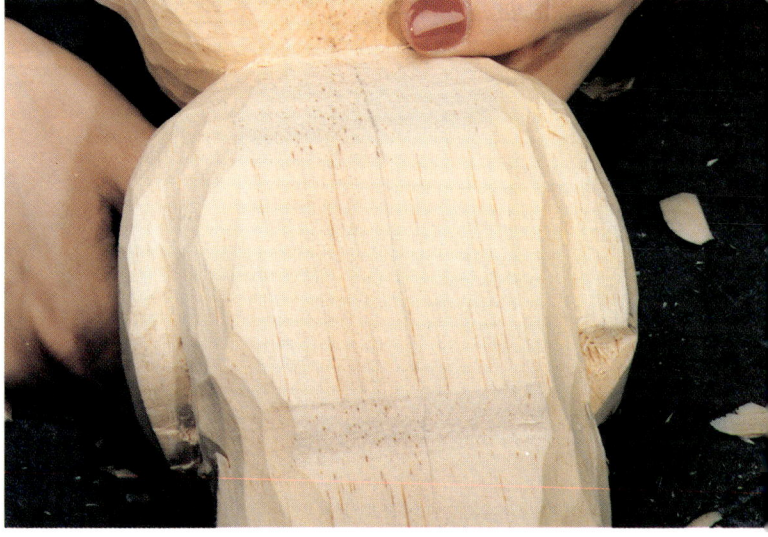

The back view.

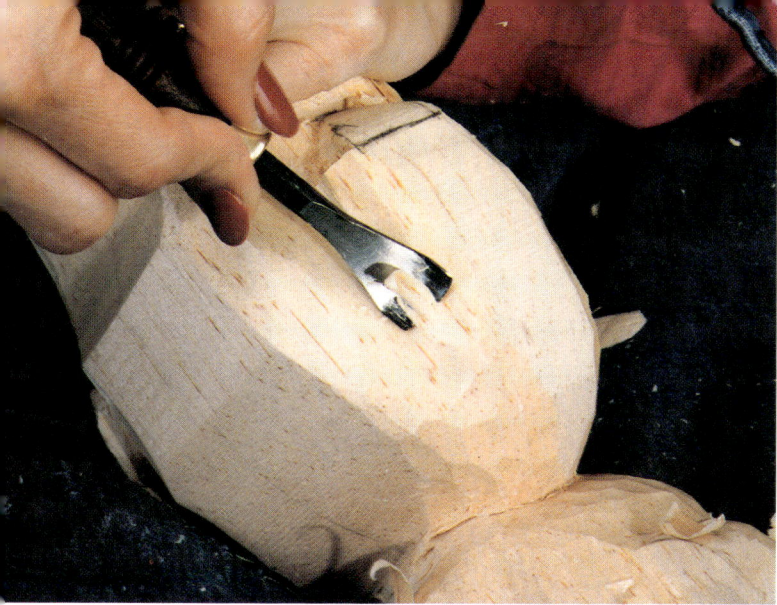

When the depth of the arms is set knock off their corners to begin shaping them.

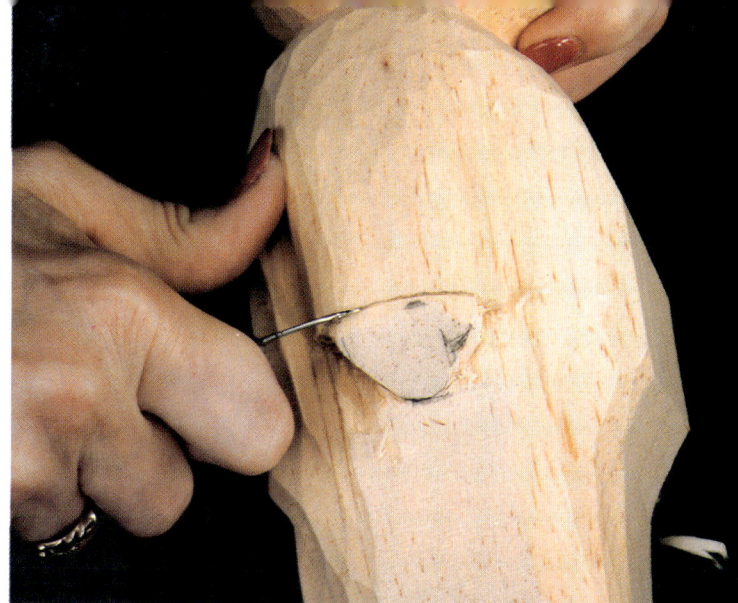

Redraw the cuff line, and score it.

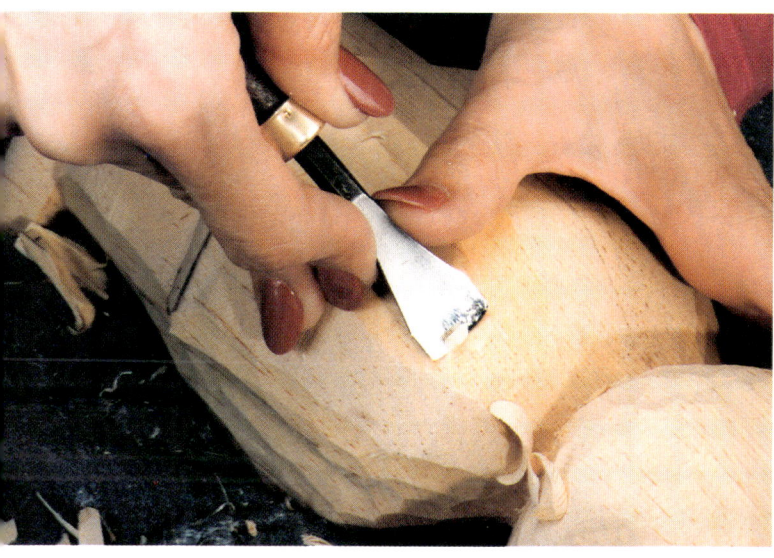

The shoulder is shaped at the same time.

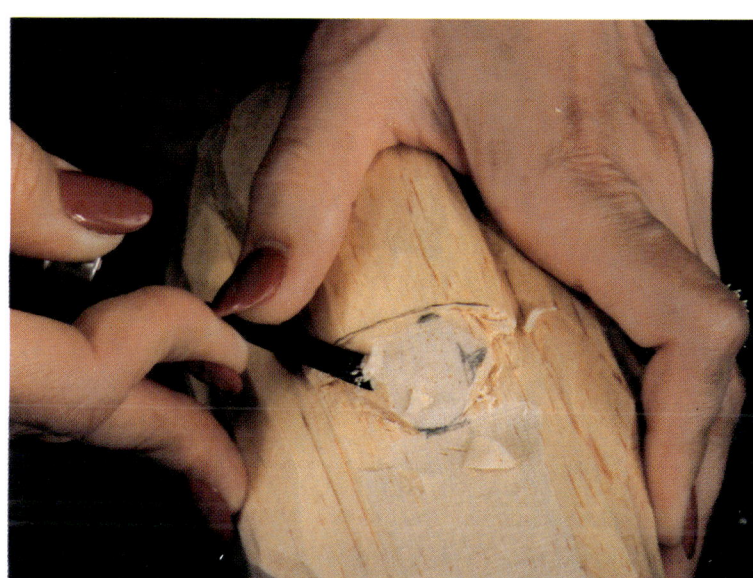

Shape the hand, first coming down from the score line...

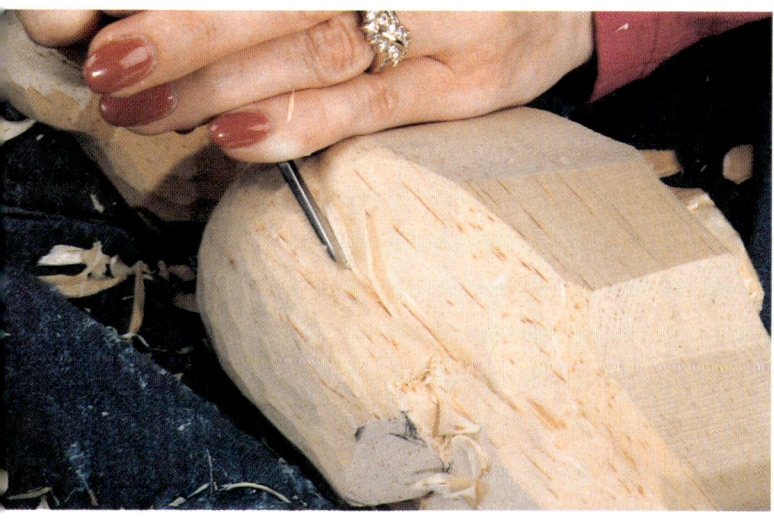

With a chisel, roll the arm under a little, making it look separate from the body.

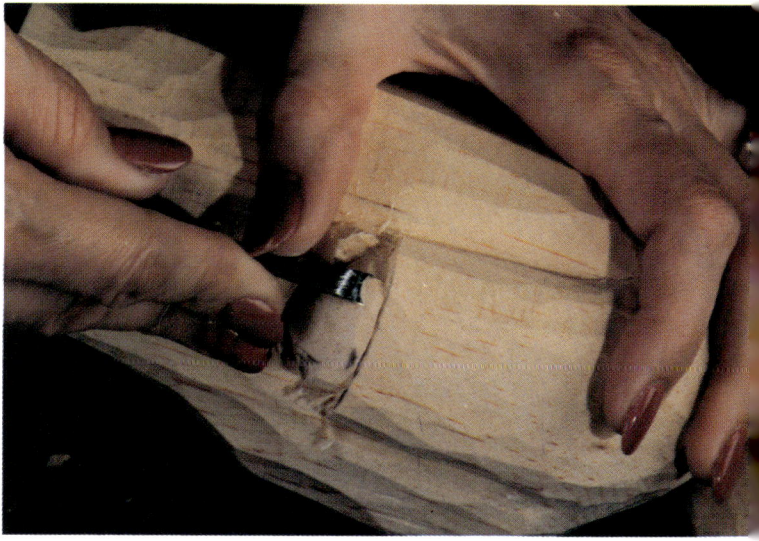

then cutting back to it.

19

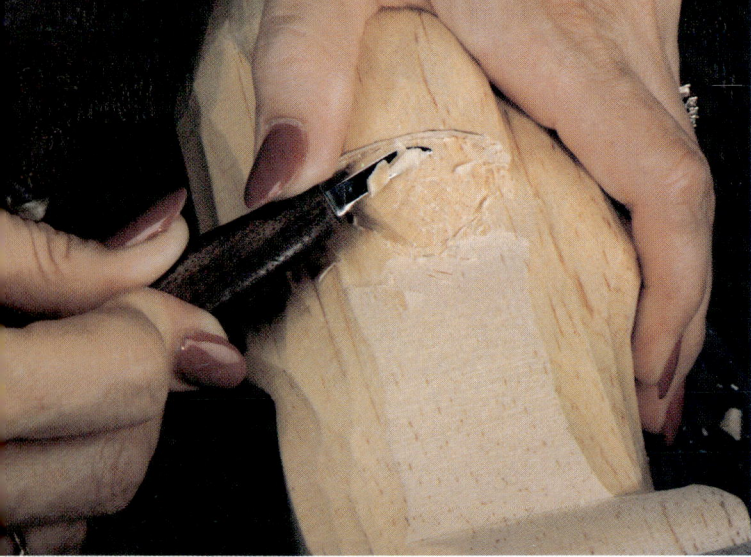

Clean up the cuts and smooth with a knife.

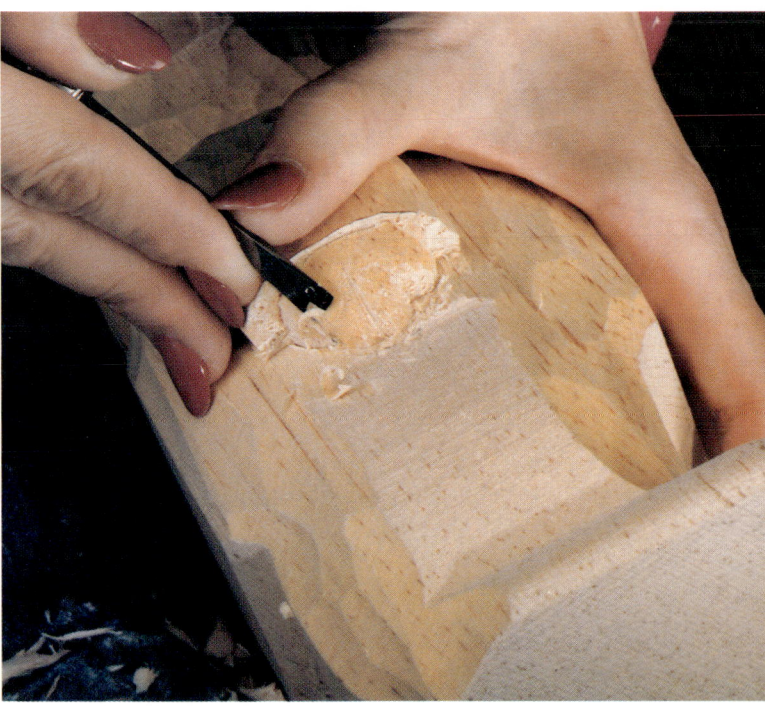

With a straight chisel, round the fingers off into the spaces.

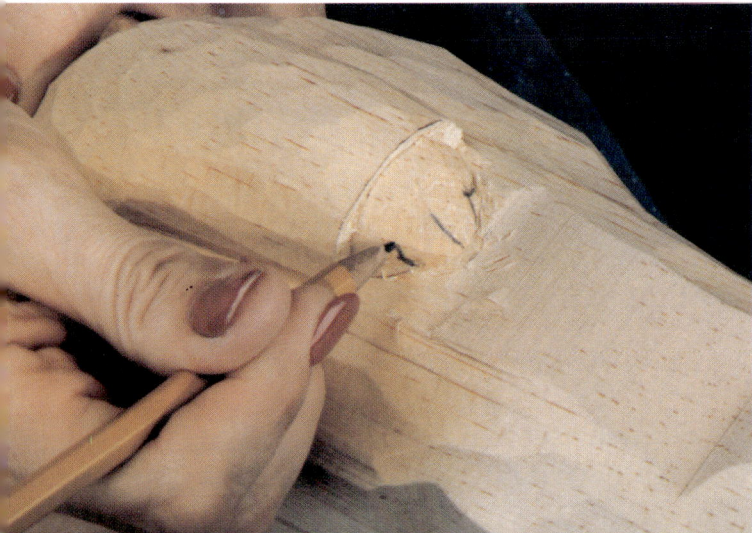

Reestablish the thumb and draw in the fingers.

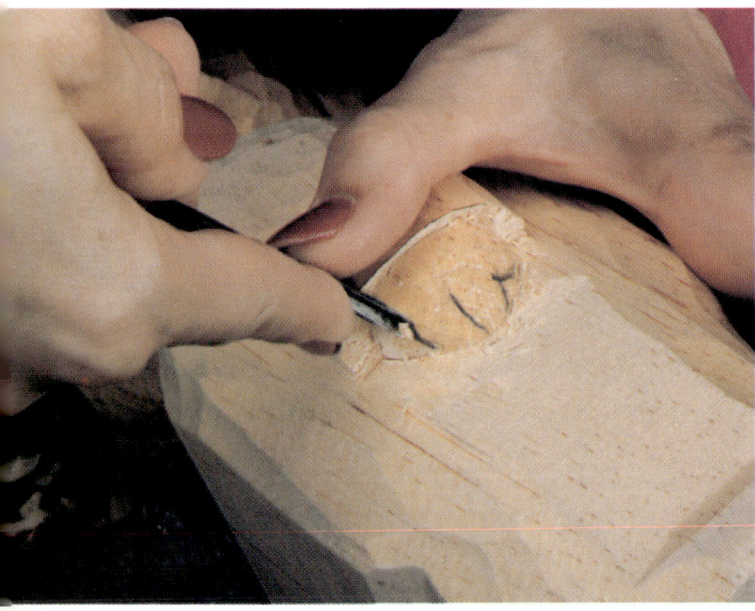

V-tool the lines between the fingers.

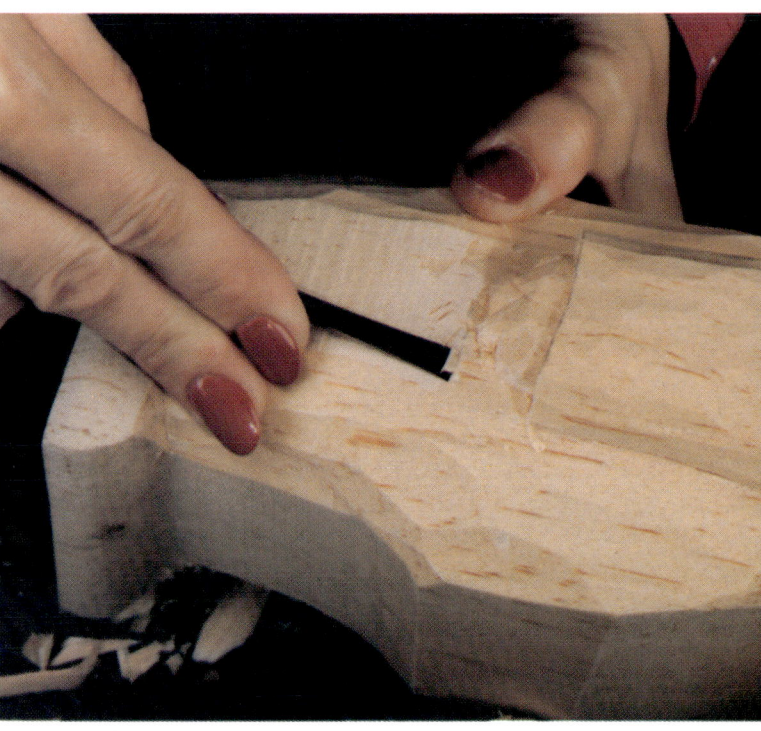

Clean up the area around the paw.

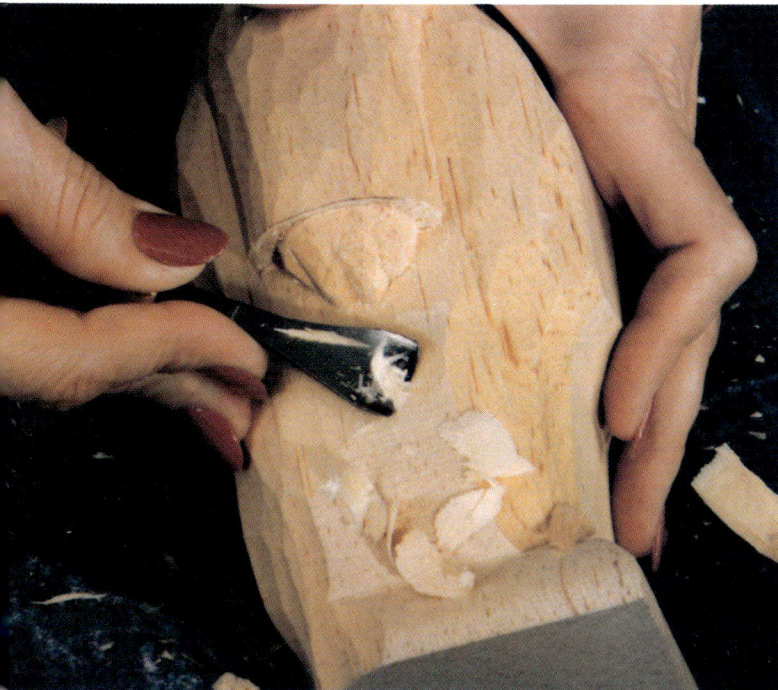

Continue cleaning the side of the leg.

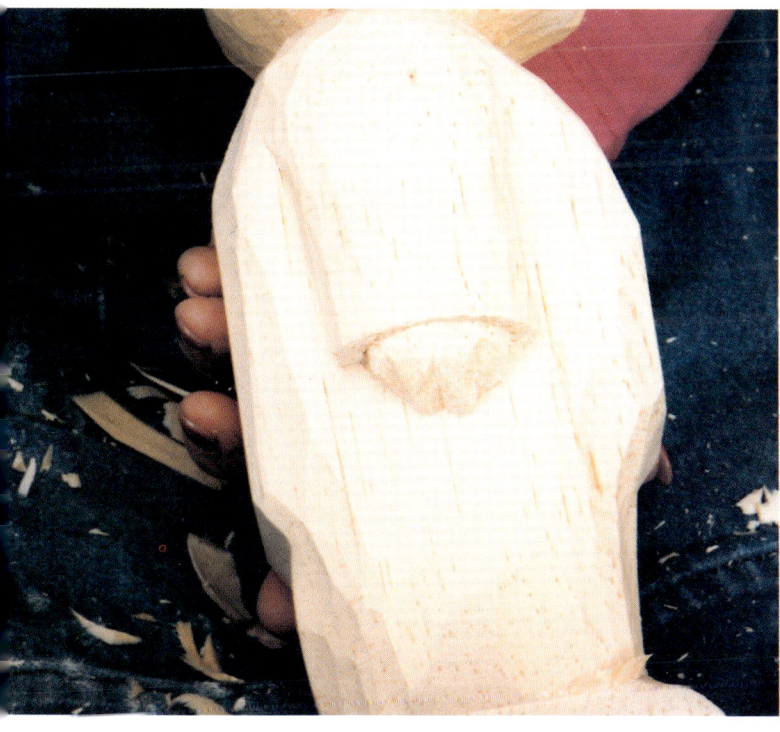

Ready to move to the other arm.

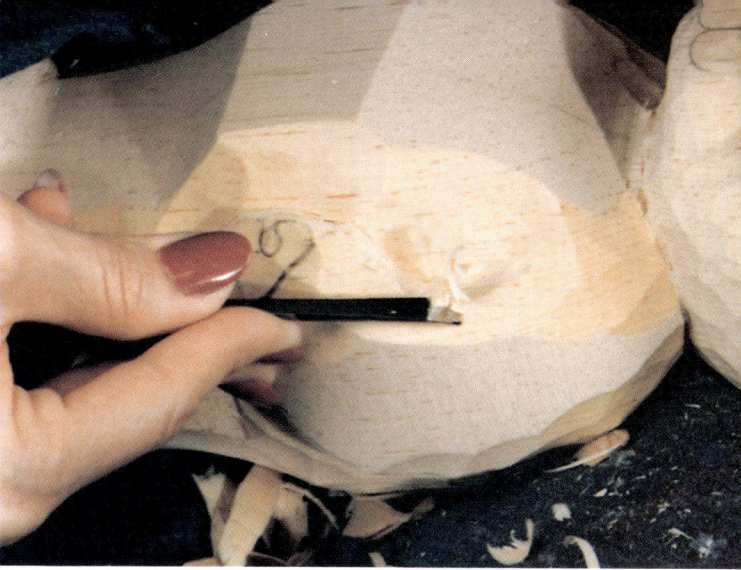

Shape the arm.

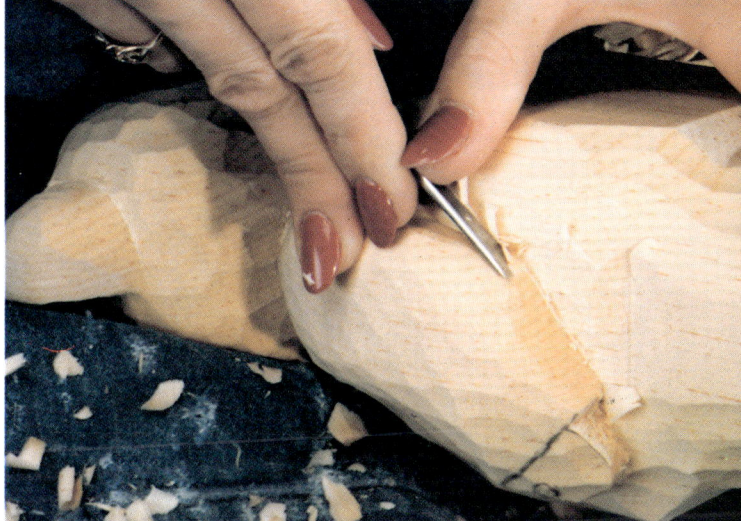

Undercut the edge where it meets the body.

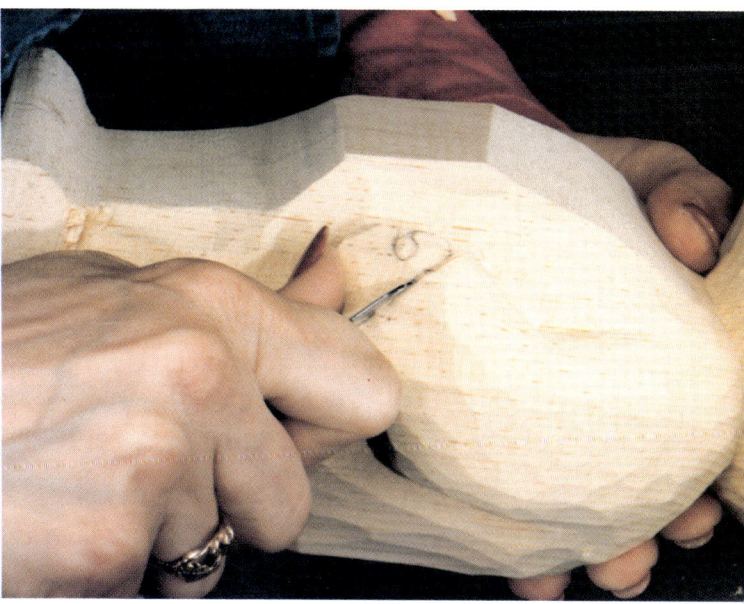

Score the cuff...

21

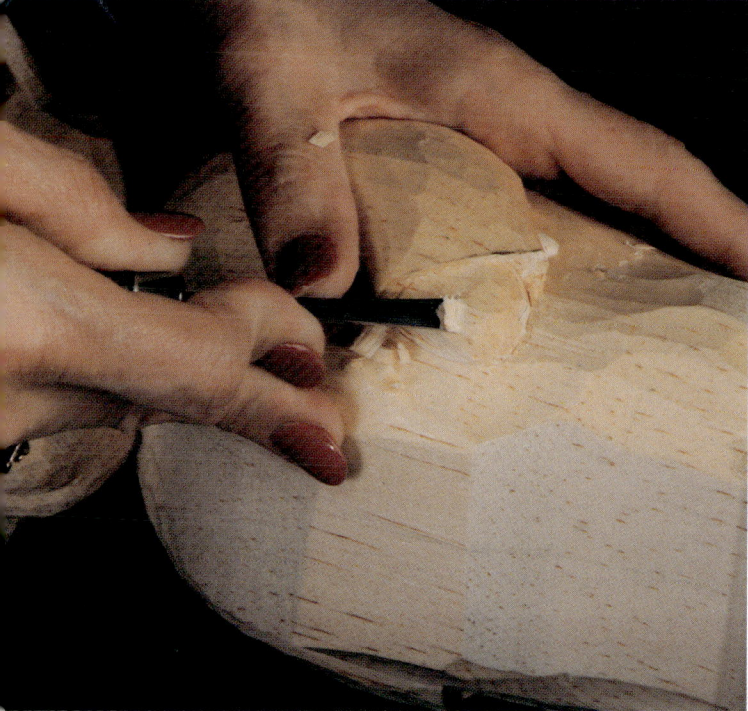

and shape paw.

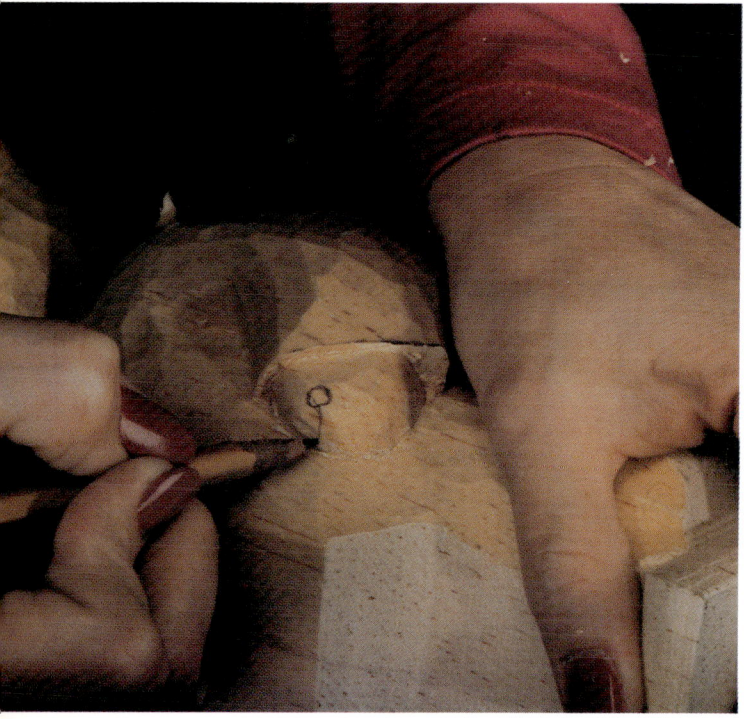

When the paw is rounded over, redraw the thumb...

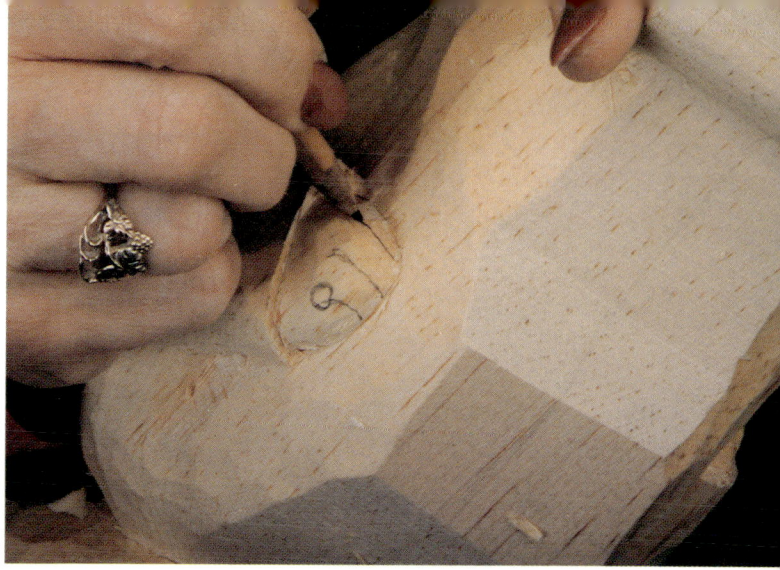

and fingers.

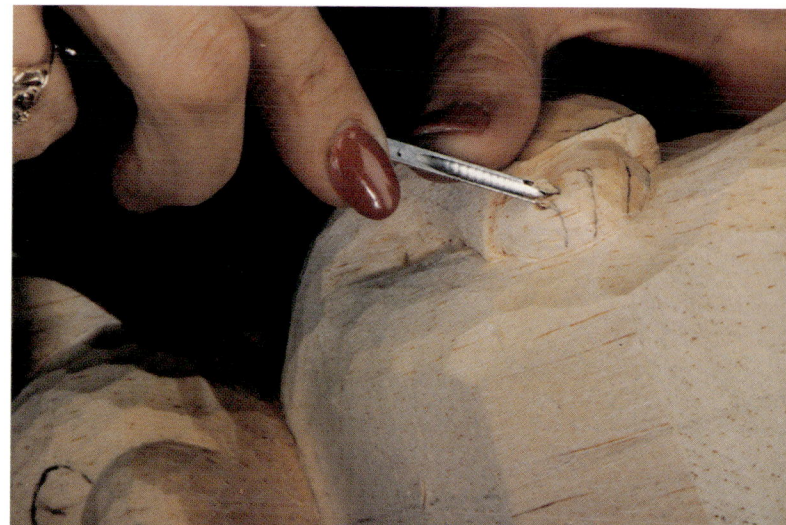

With a small gouge carve a round hole at the space between the thumb and finger.

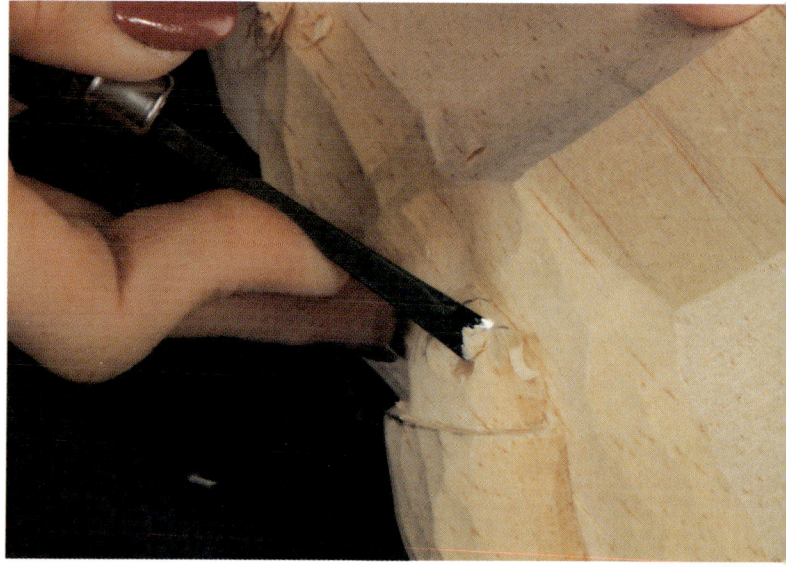

Carve the thumb.

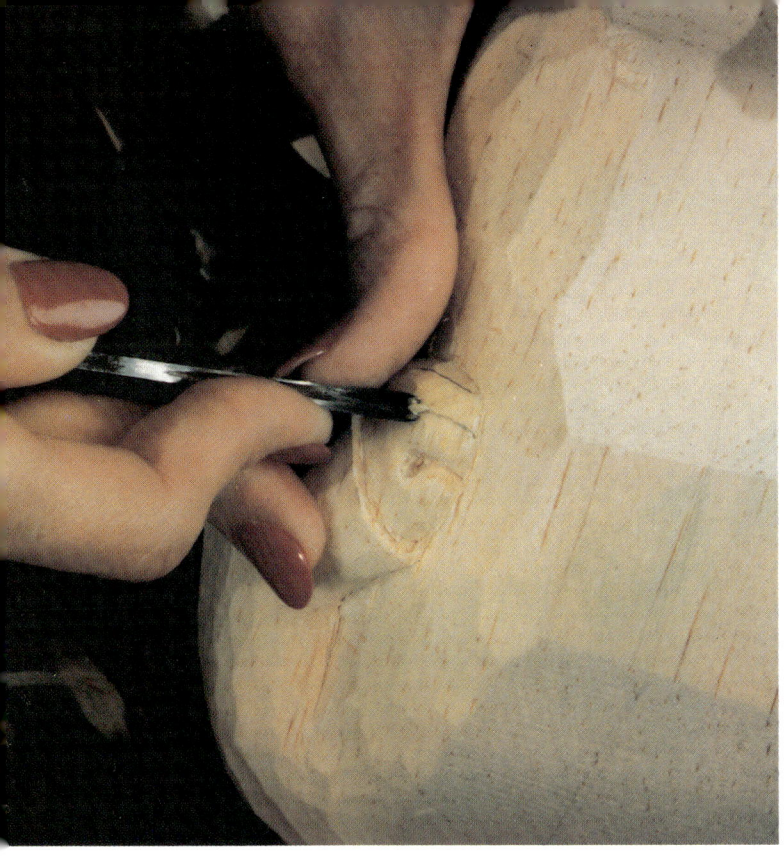

V-tool between the fingers.

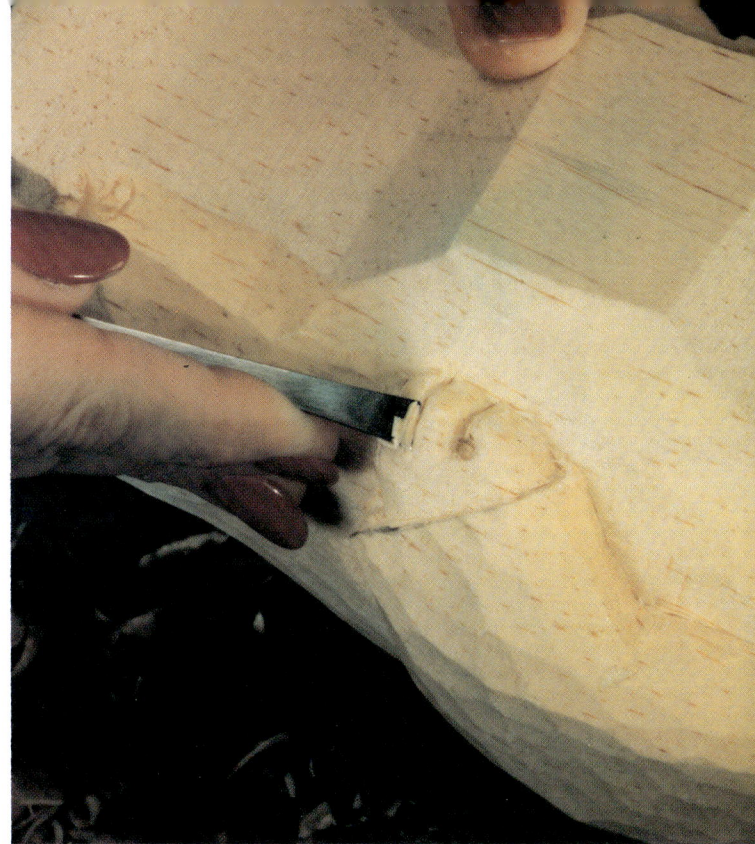

Shape the fingers.

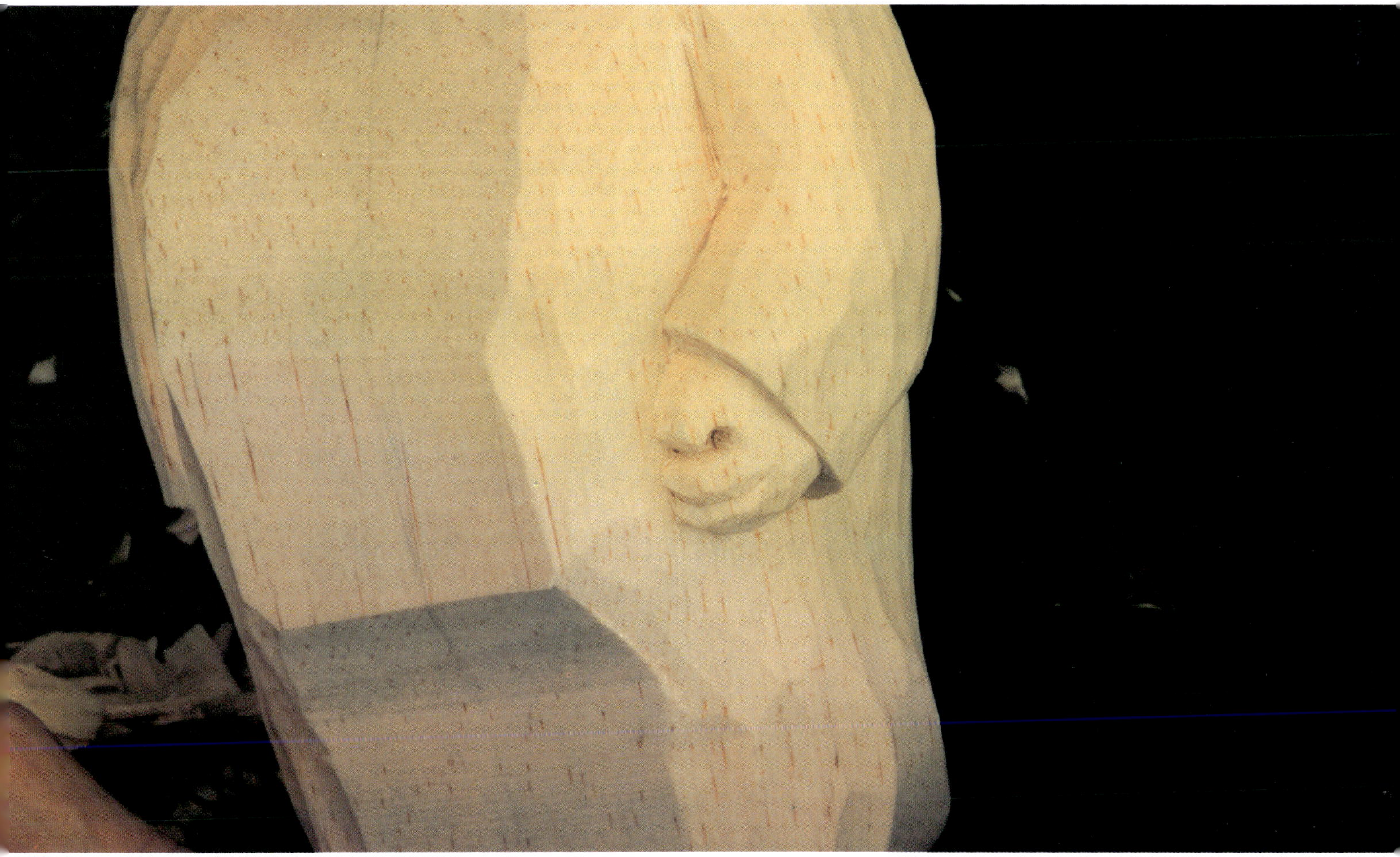

The finished hand.

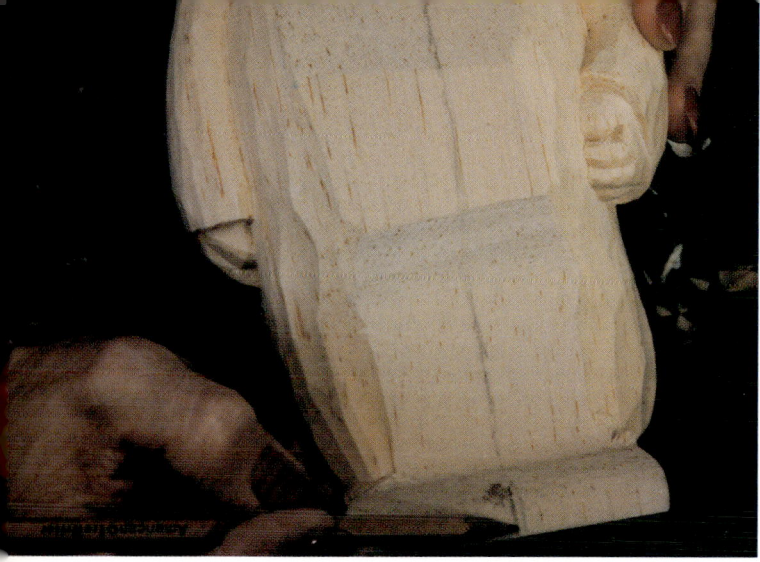

Reestablish the midline before shaping the body.

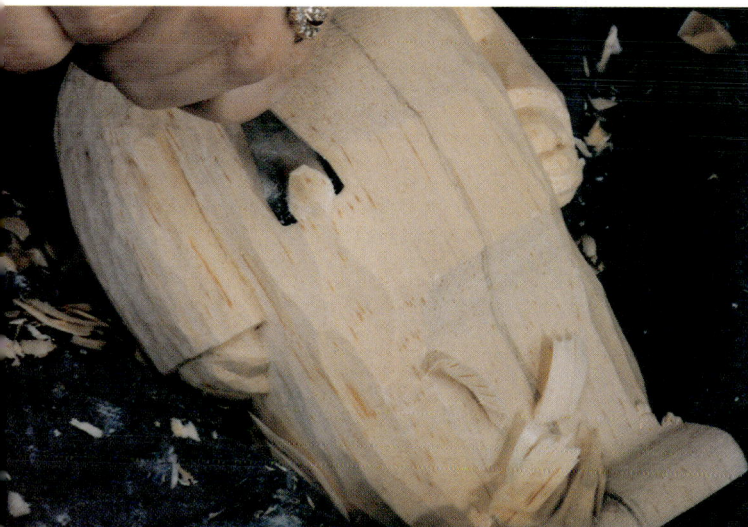

The fattest part of the body is the stomach at the midline. I need to shape the body so it flows out to that point.

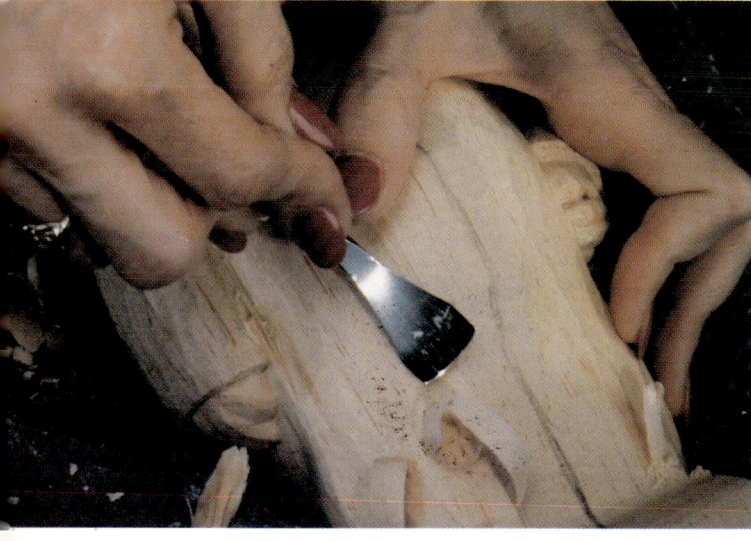

As you work on the body keep an eye out for symmetry. If you need to make adjustments to the body, do it as you go.

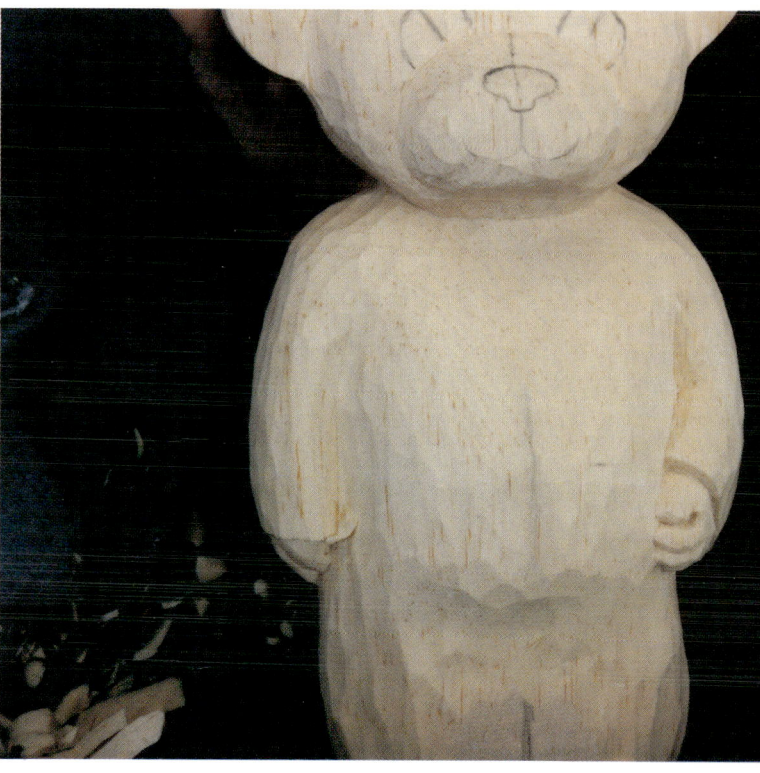

When the basic shape and symmetry is set, smooth the body for this result.

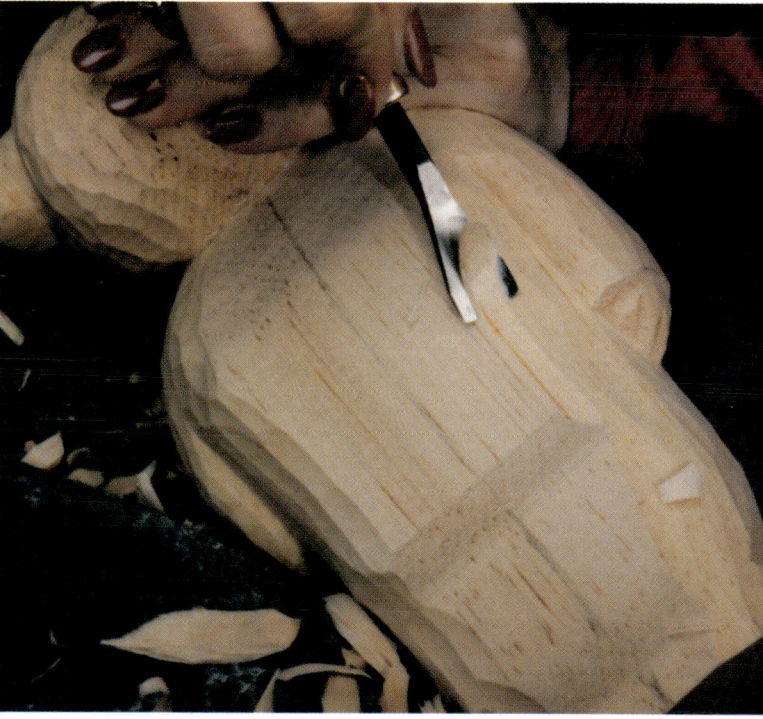

Shape the back.

24

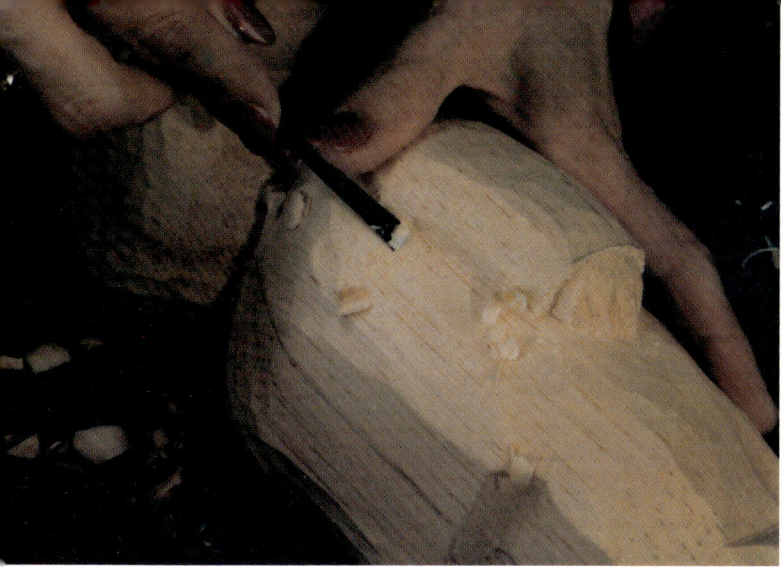

The arms may need to be deeper to get the shape you want.

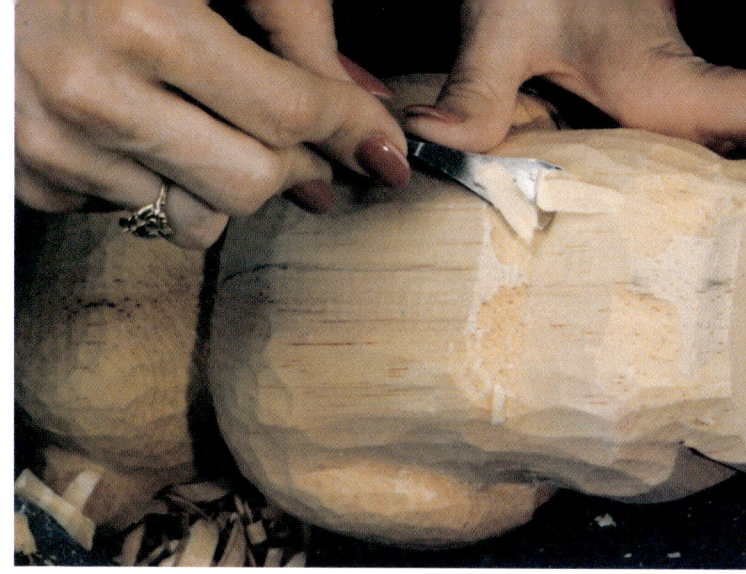

The transition between the buns and the legs should be more of a scoop than a line.

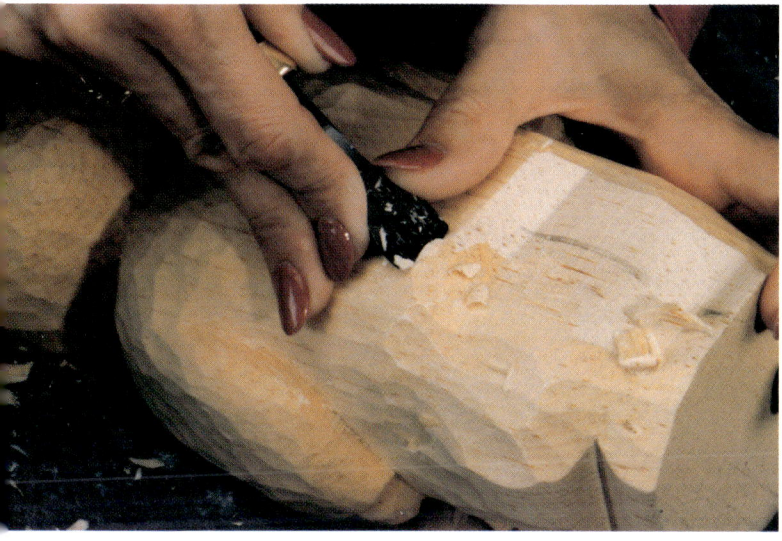

Continue rounding the bare...er bear buns...

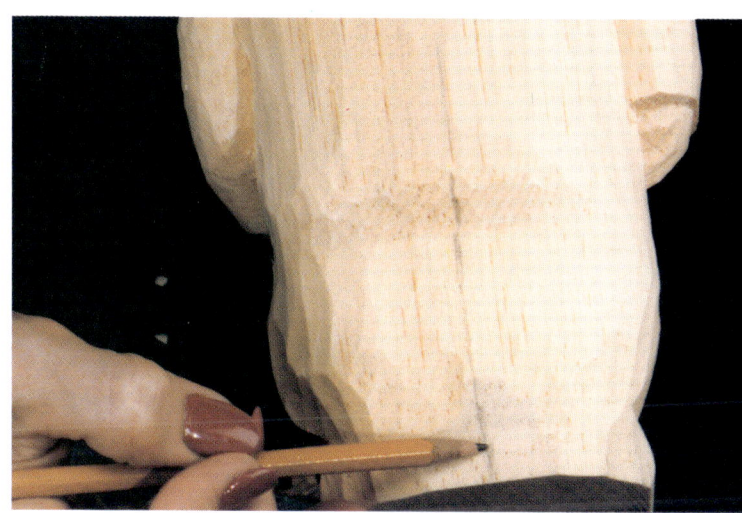

Redraw the center line in the back of the legs.

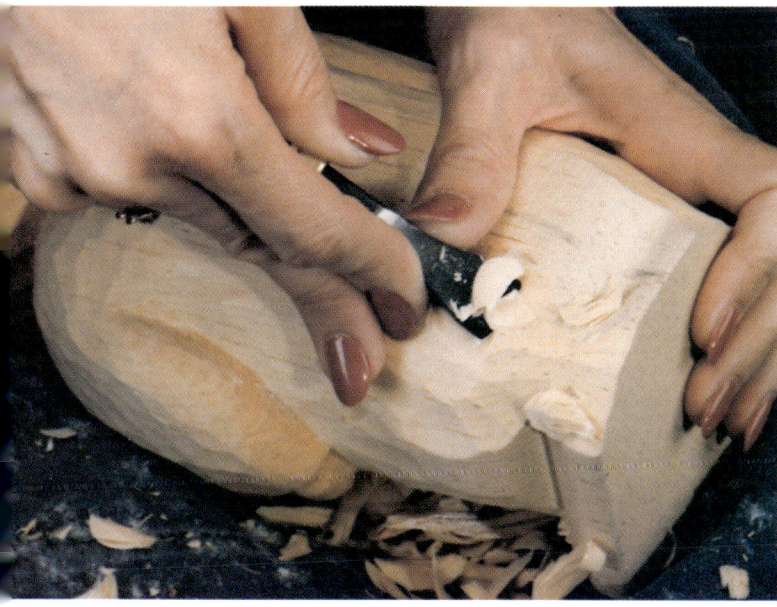

and the legs.

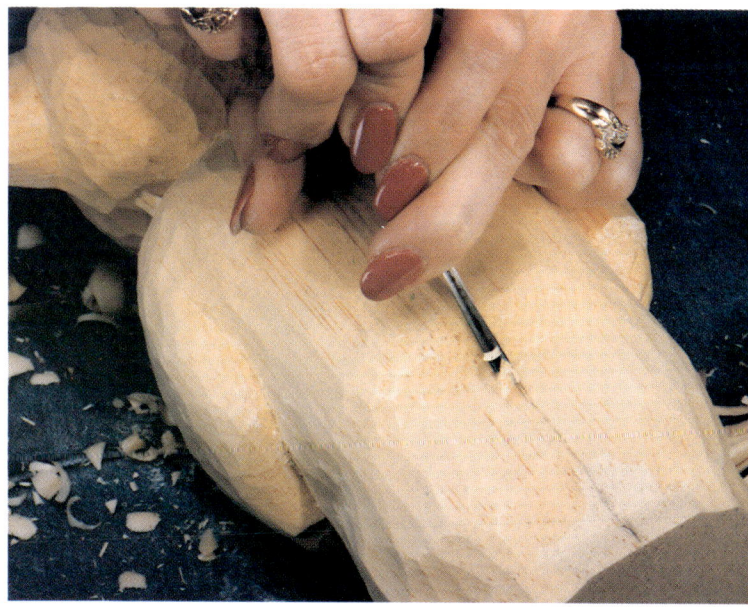

Separate the legs with a v-tool.

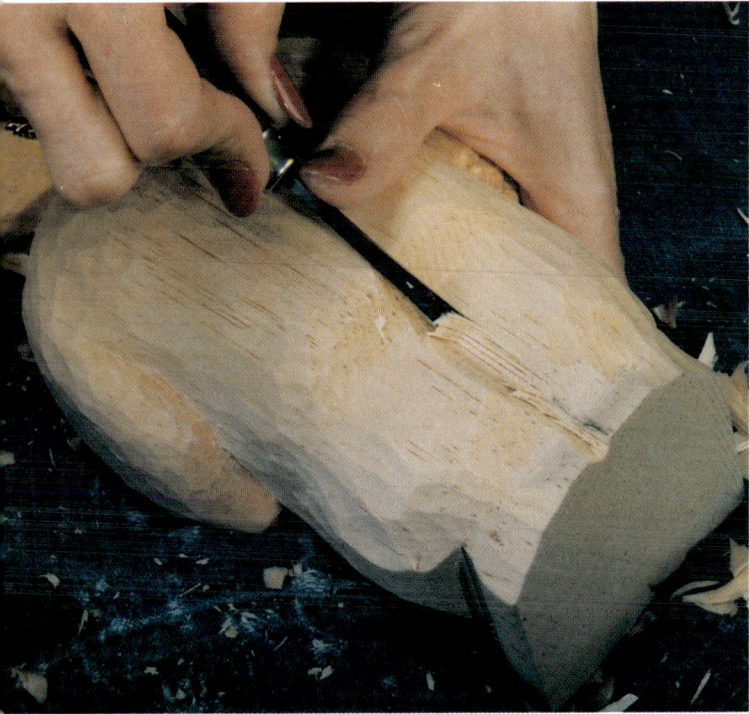

Deepen the separation with a chisel.

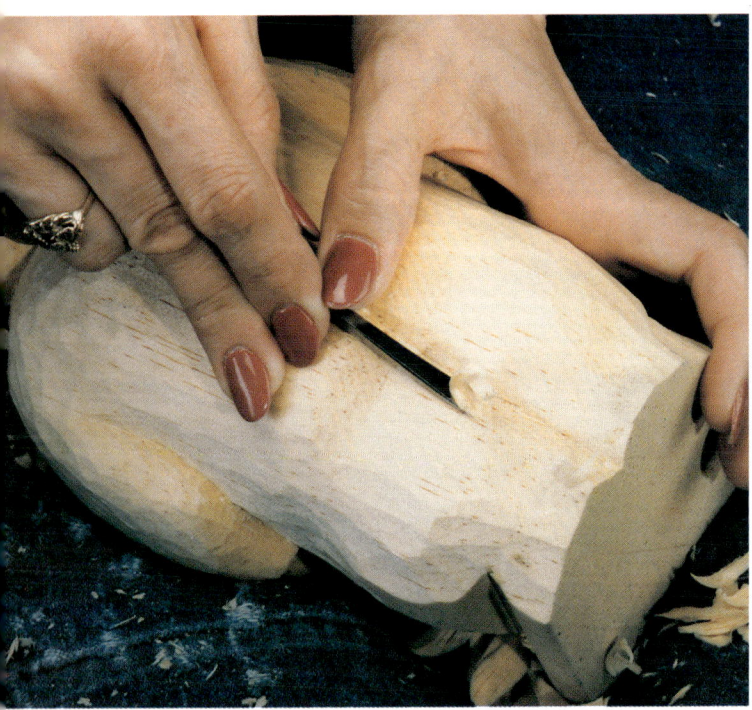

Work your way out from the separation to shape the legs.

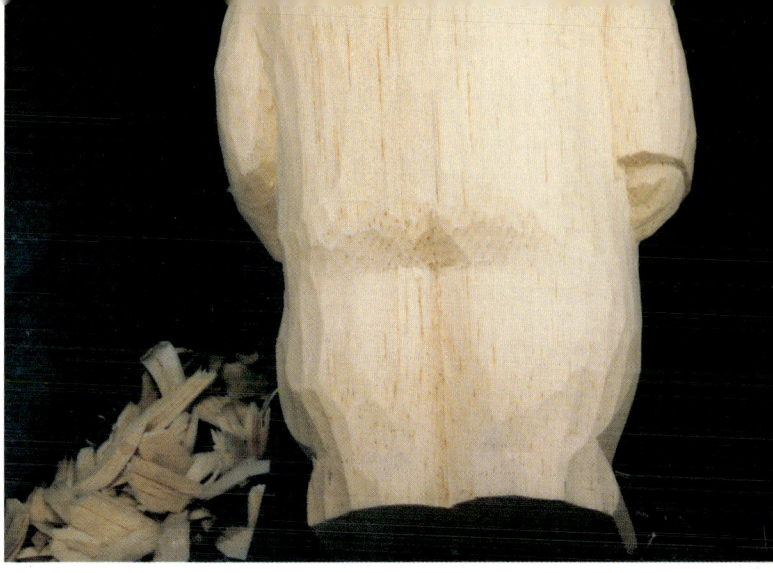

Progress.

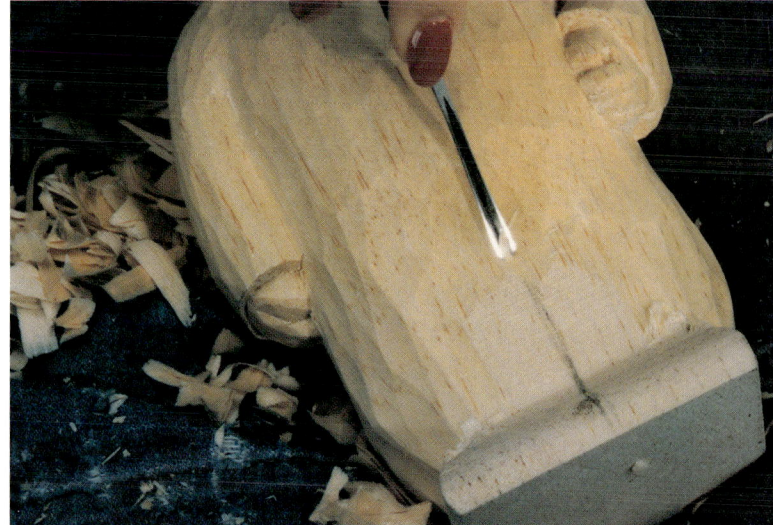

The same steps are used on the front. Cut the separation with a v-tool.

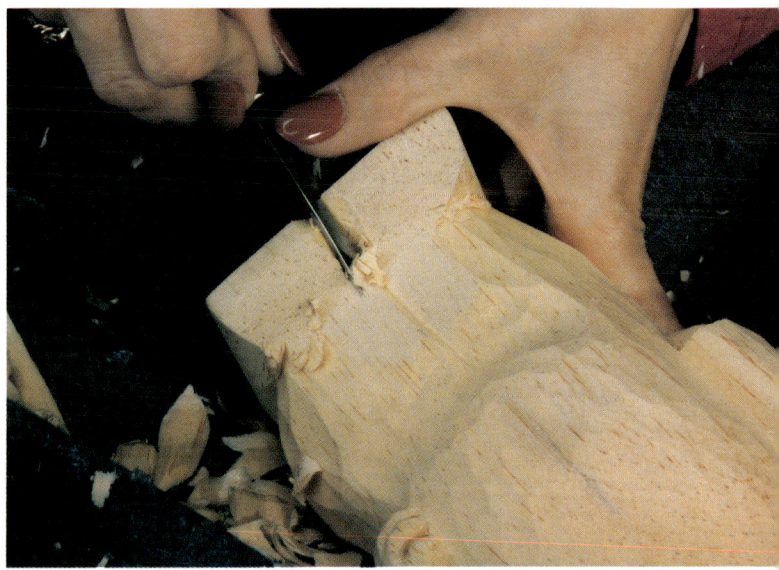

Deepen it with a chisel.

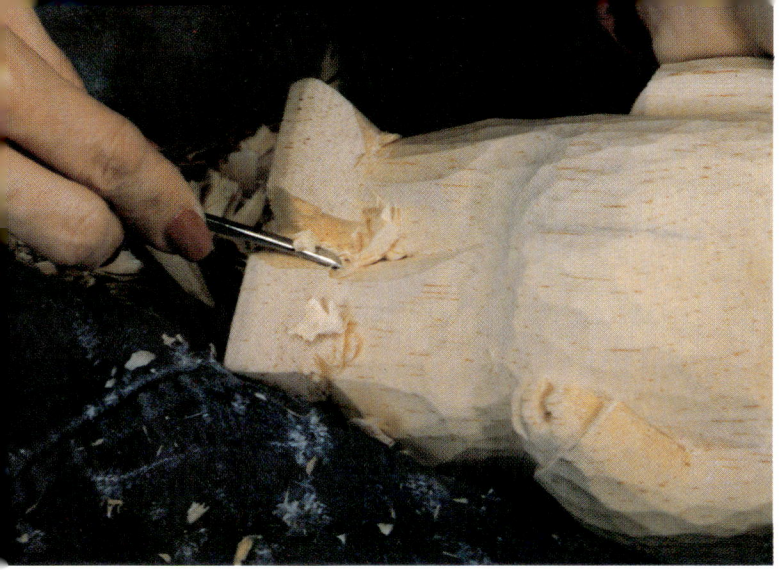

Continue the separation between the feet.

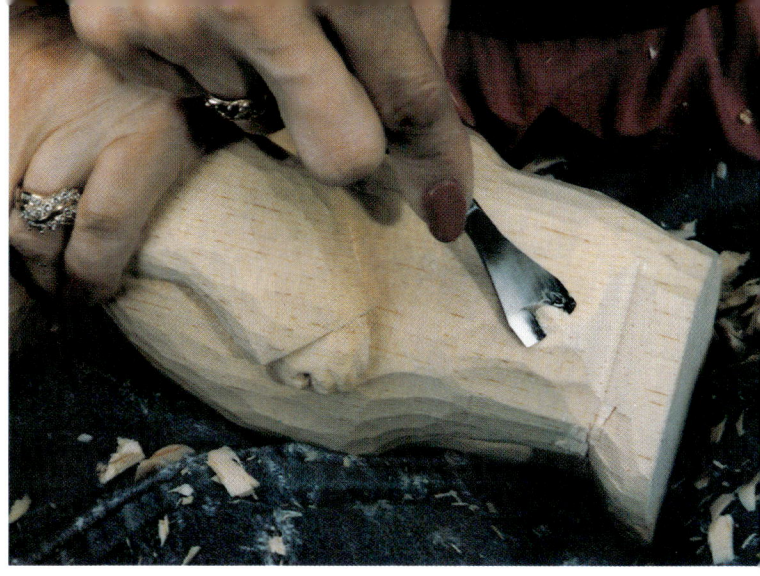

Shape the sides of the legs. If you have any bulges, like I do here, take them away.

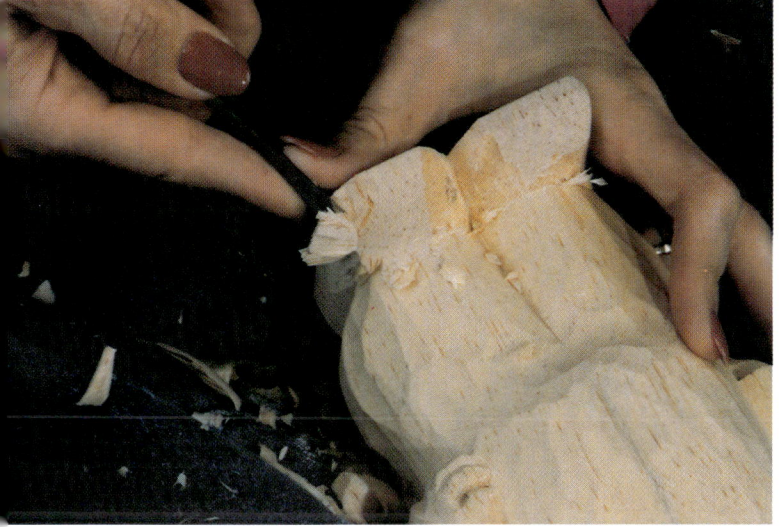

Pop off the corners of the feet...

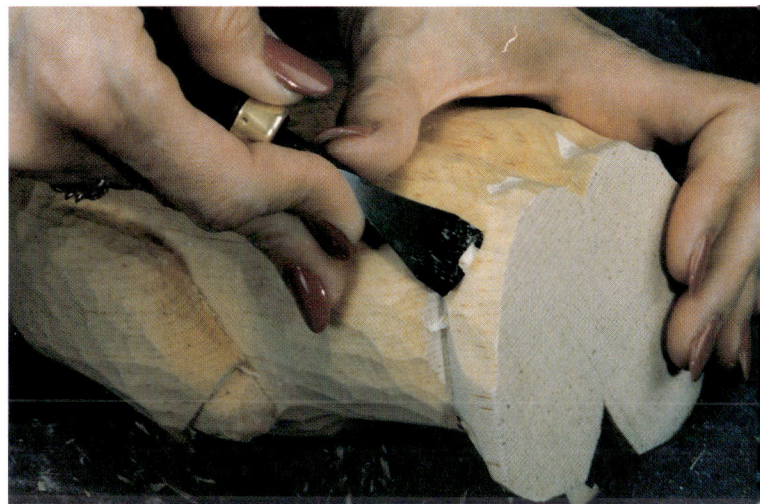

The heels will be narrower than the toes.

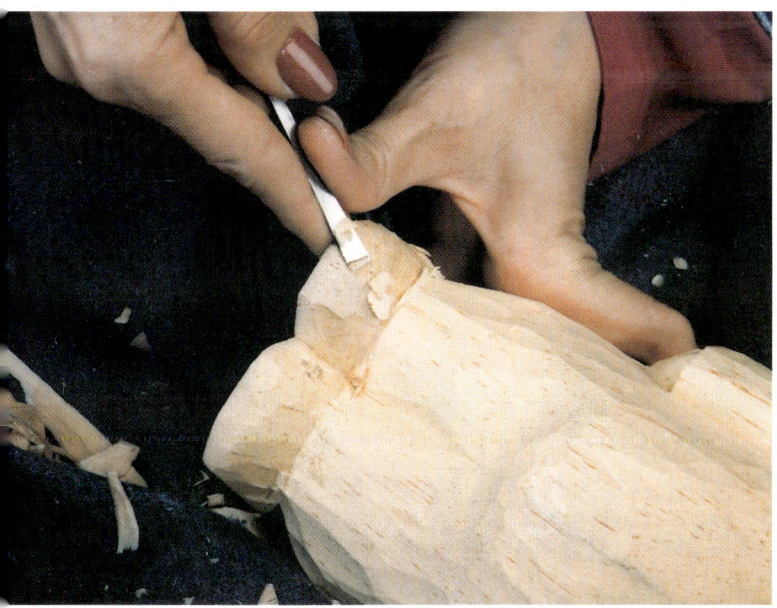

and round off the toes.

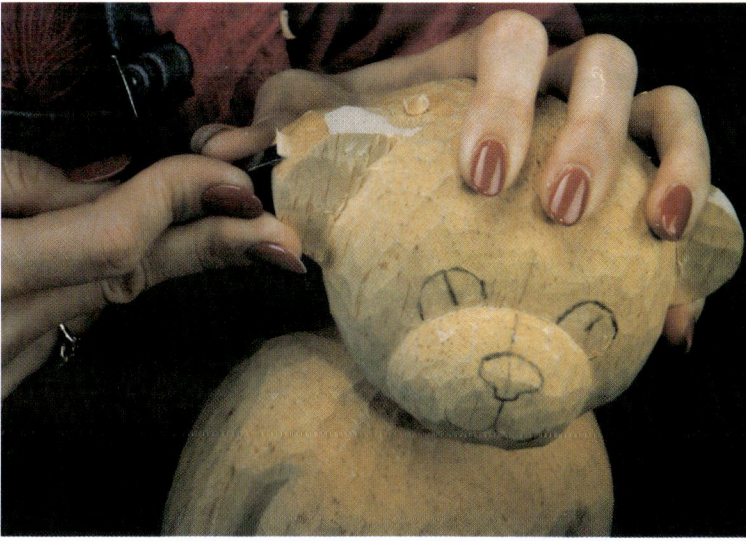

Look the piece over carefully. You want the overall shapes and proportions to be correct before dressing him. This ear was a little big, so I am reducing it.

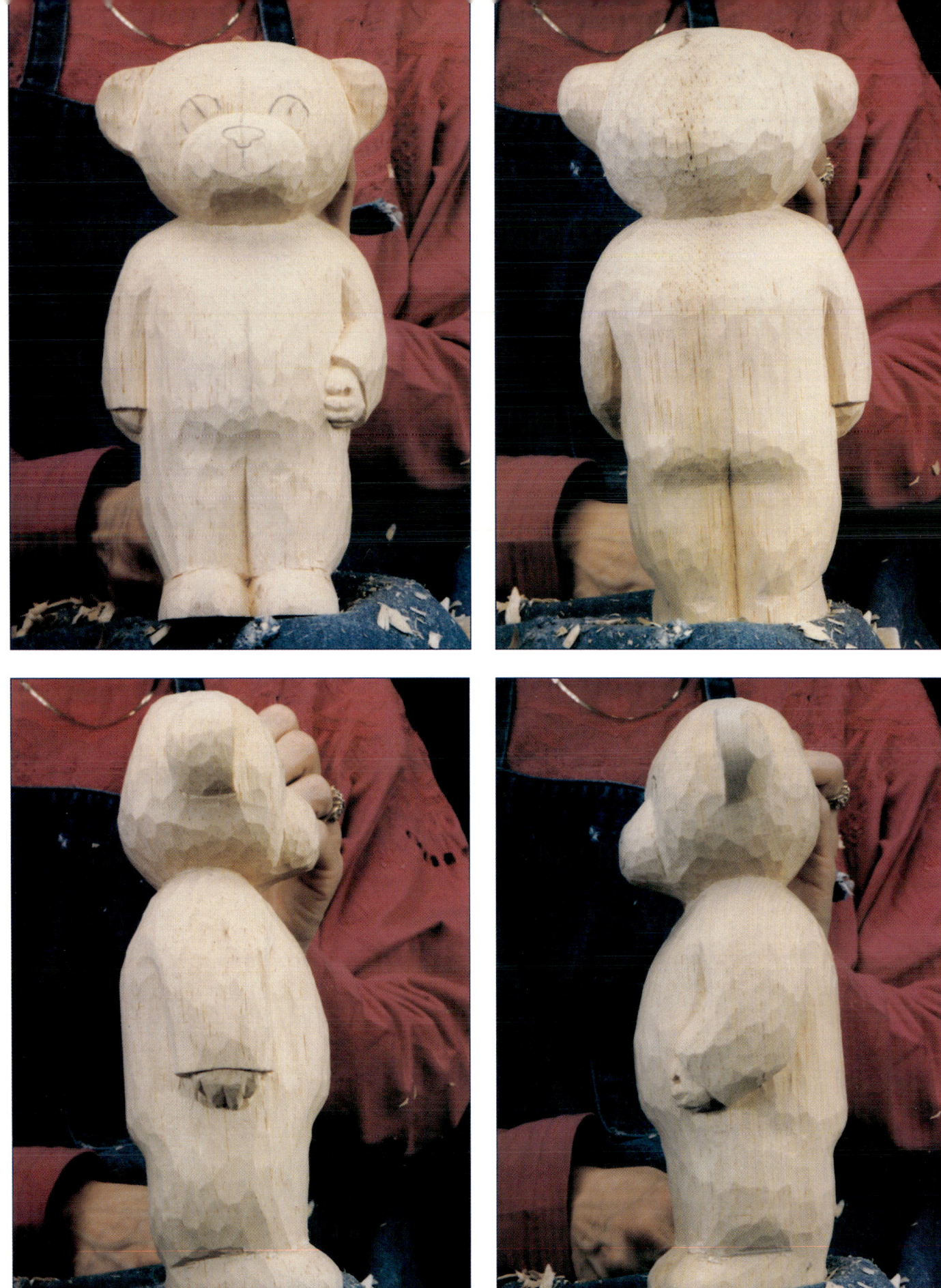

Ready for dressing. The body gives the clothing its shape. This is why the clothing is done last.

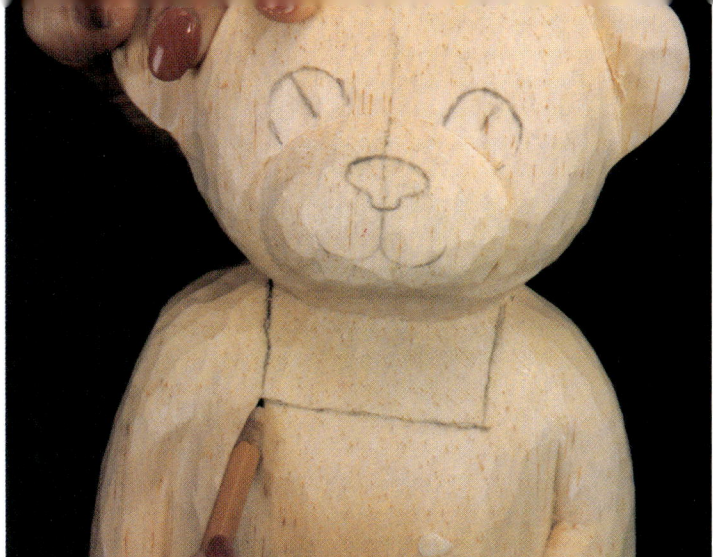

Draw the top of the bib...

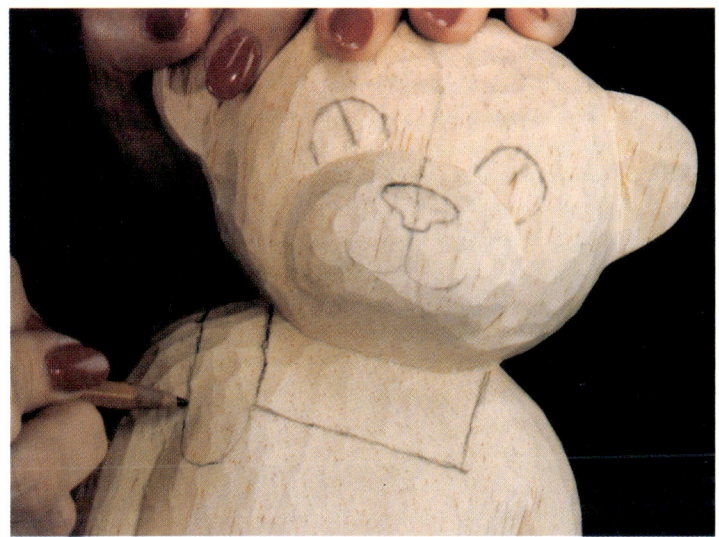

and the shoulder straps.

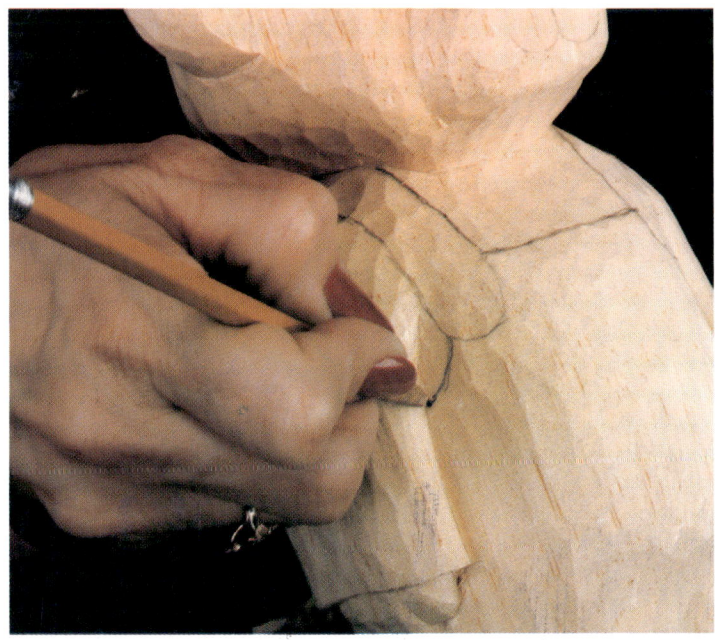

Draw the line of the bib as it goes under the arm.

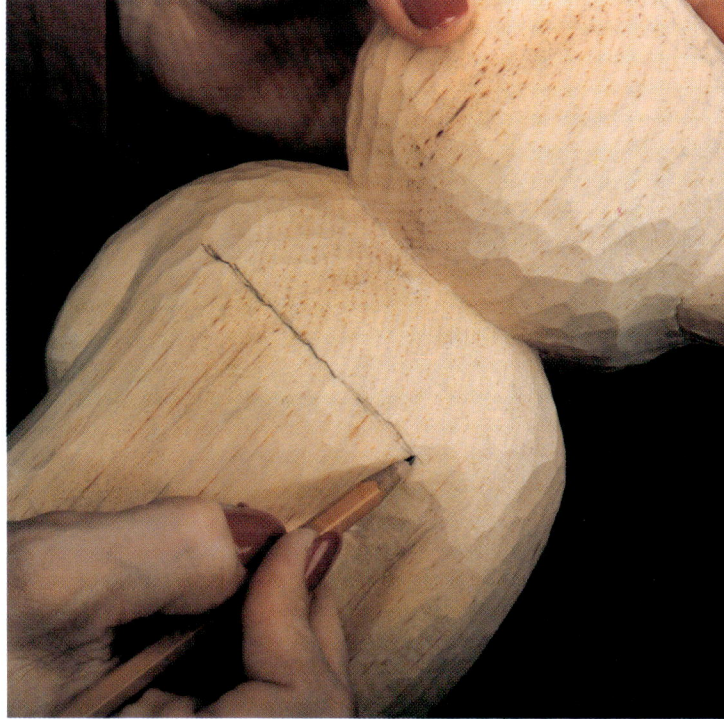

Draw the back of the bib.

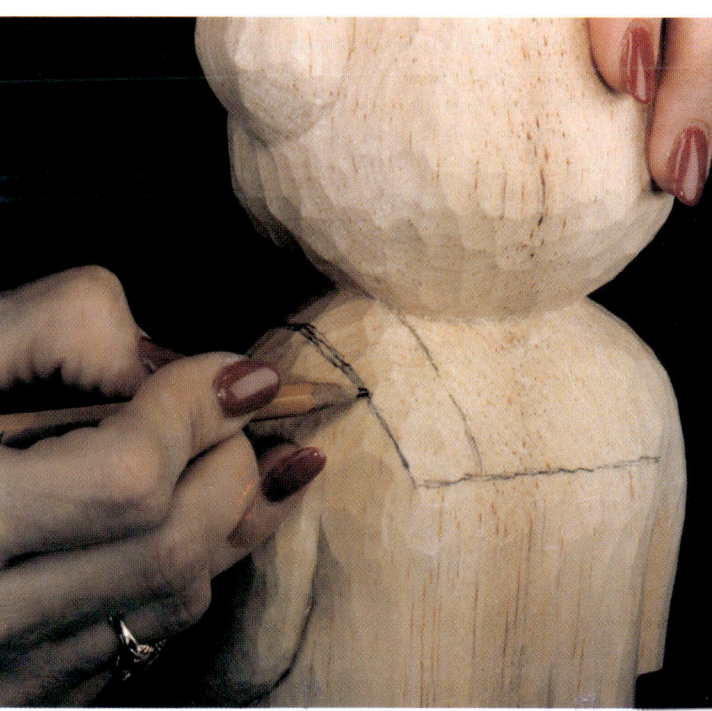

Continue the strap over the shoulder.

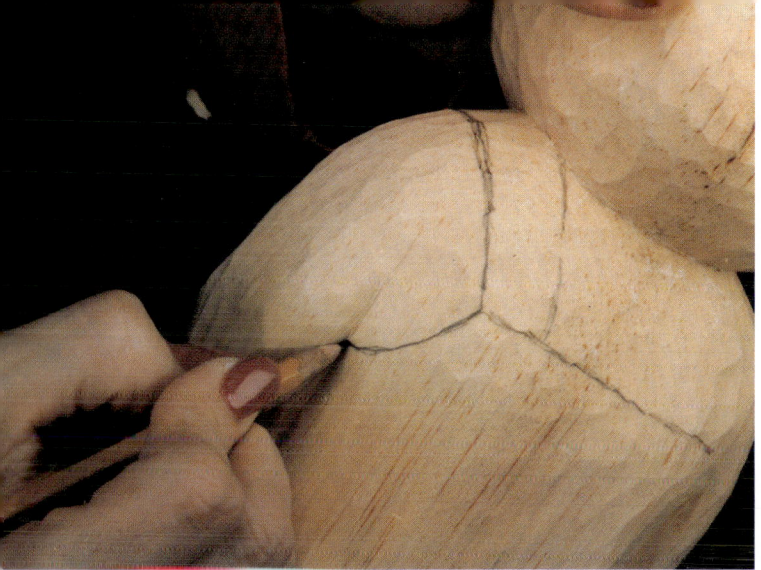

Complete the line of the bib going under the arm.

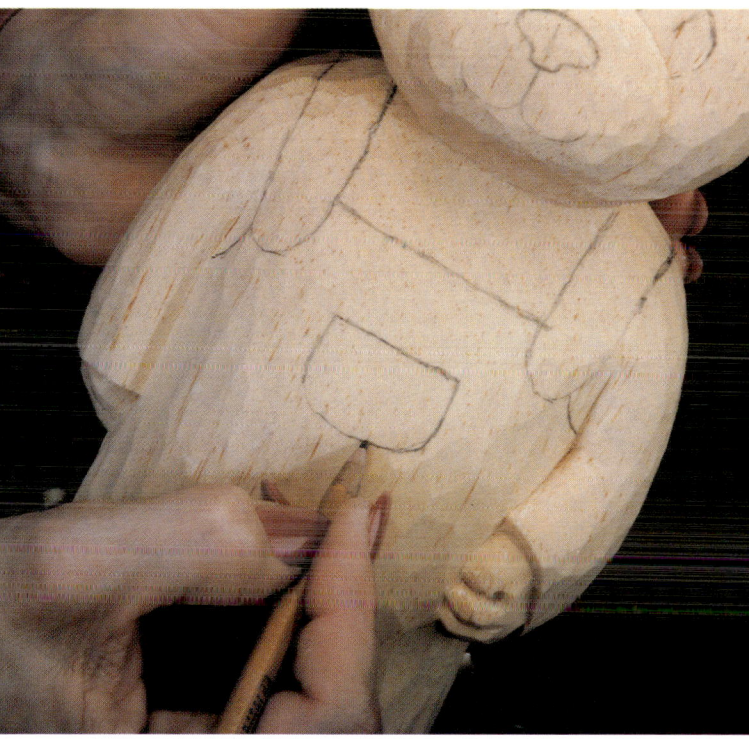

Draw another pocket on the front of the bib.

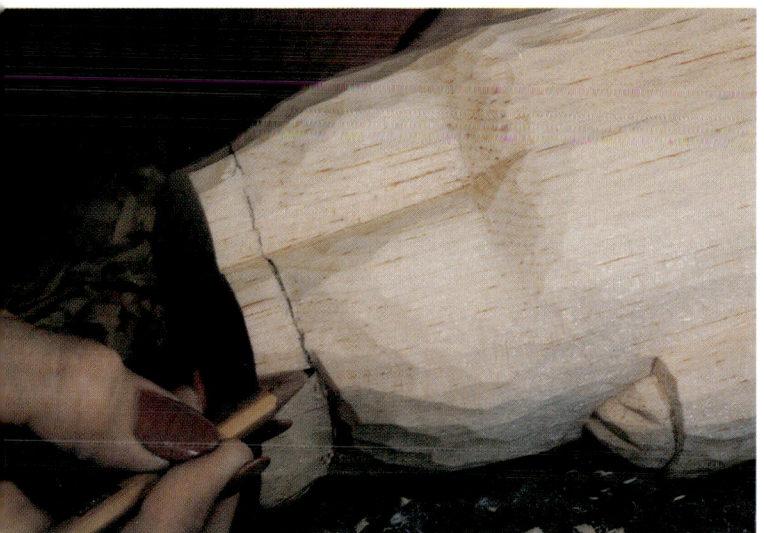

Draw the bottom of the overalls...

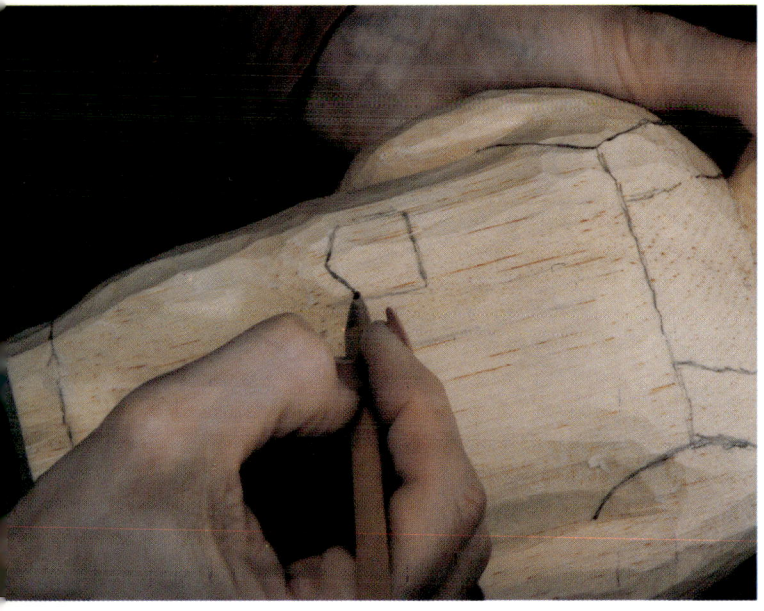

and a little pocket on the back.

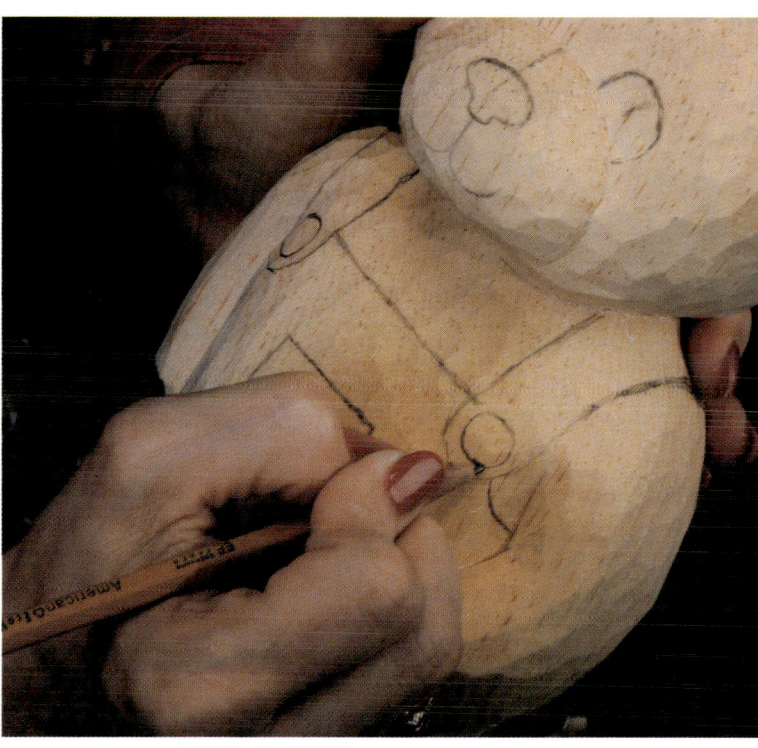

Make some big old buttons, as every well-dressed bear should have.

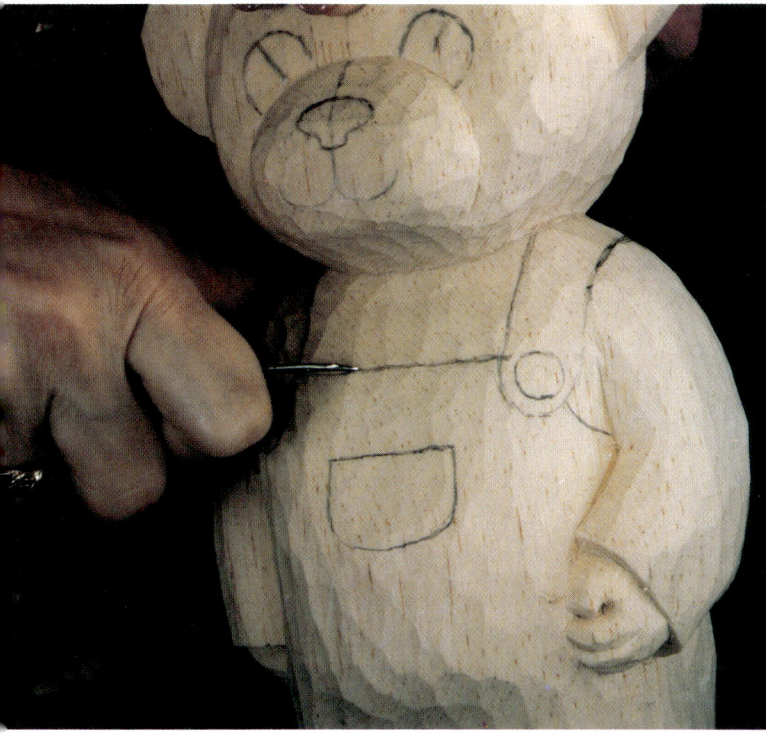

Score shallowly on all the lines. All that is necessary is to define a thin piece of fabric.

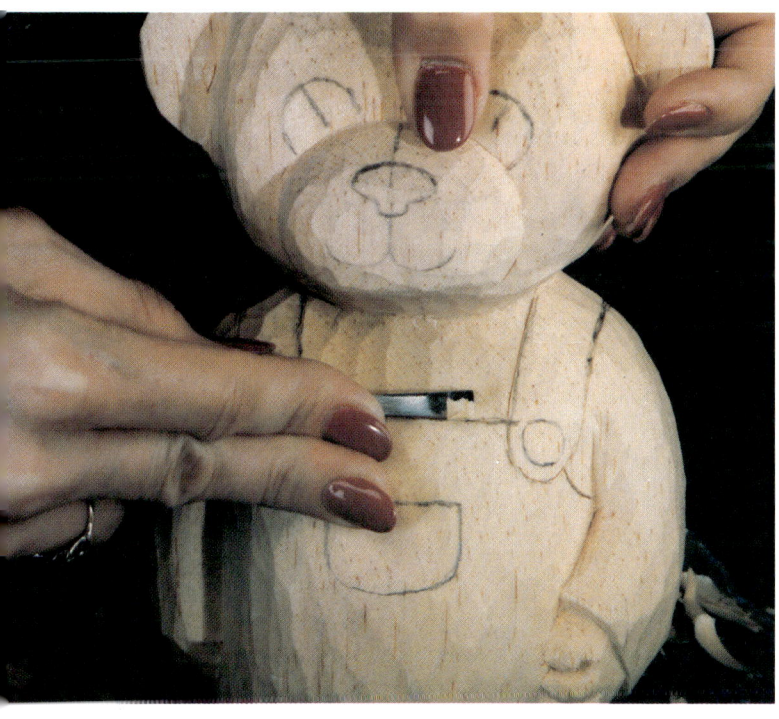

Slice along the side of the score to drop the shirt layer under the bib.

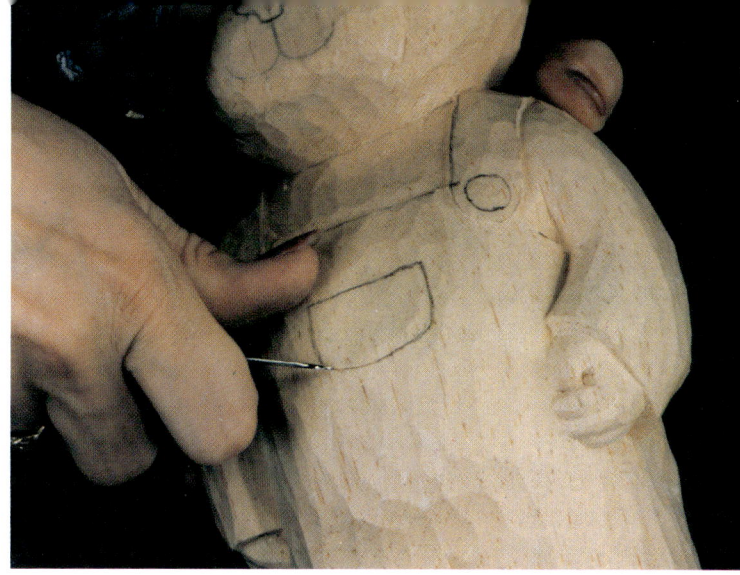

Do the same with the pockets.

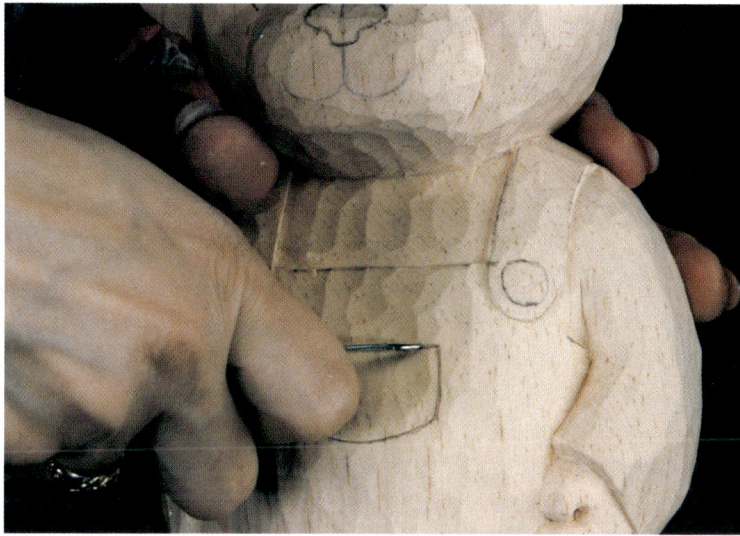

On the pocket, the opening at the top has a nice crisp edge...

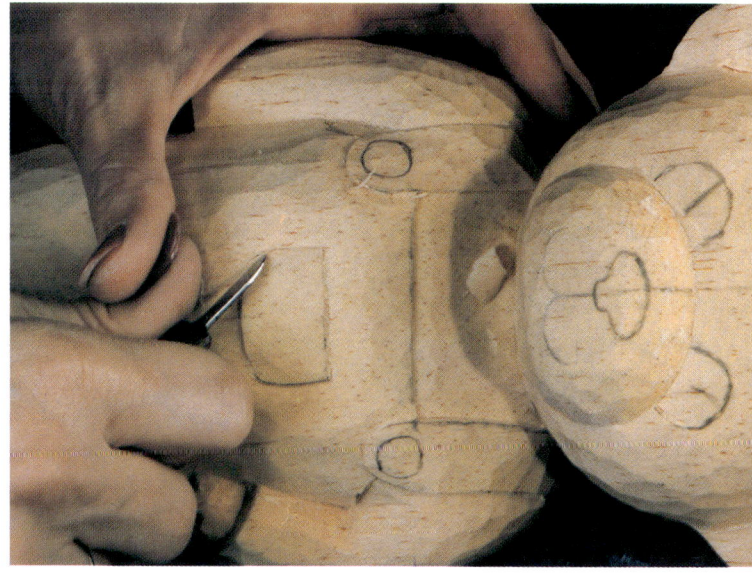

but the other three sides are rolled under and need to be slightly rounded.

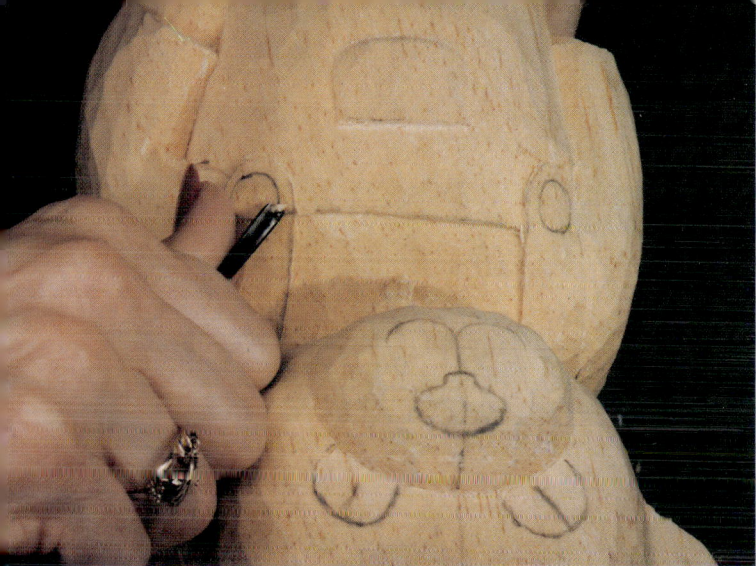

V-tool around the buttons.

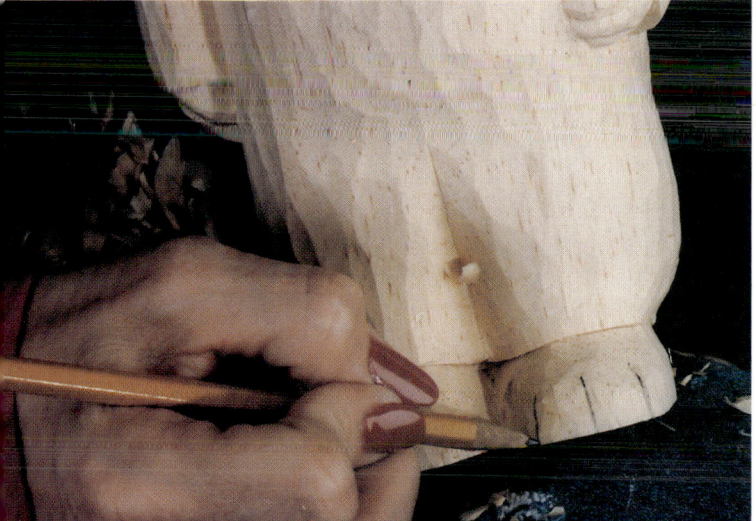

Draw the toes.

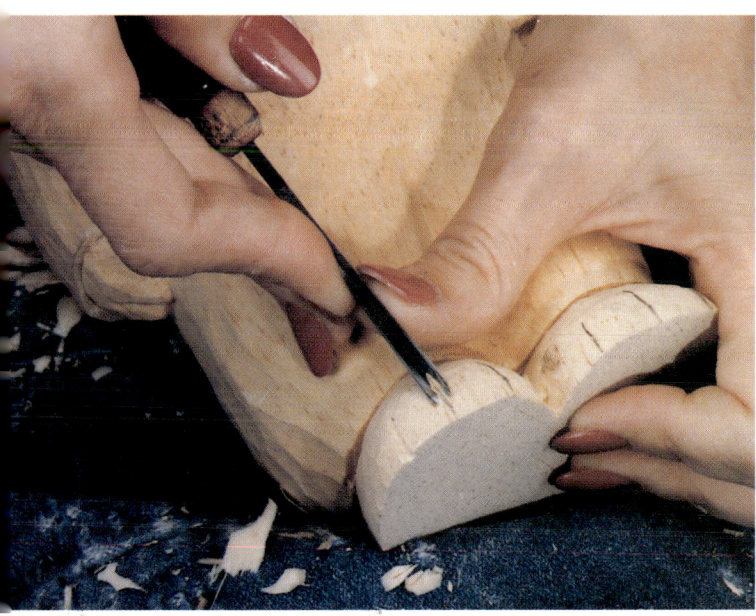

Separate them with a v-tool...

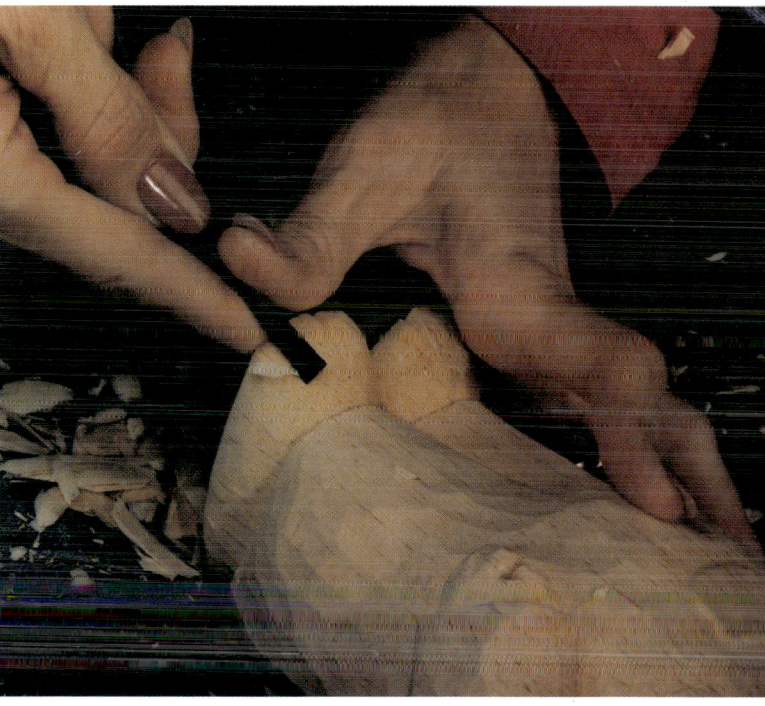

and round the toes into the separations.

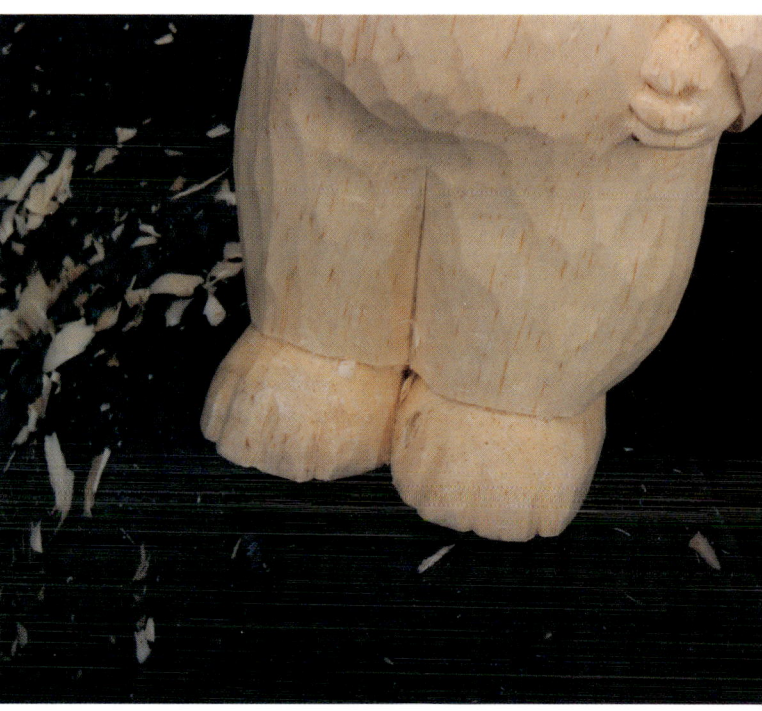

The result.

32

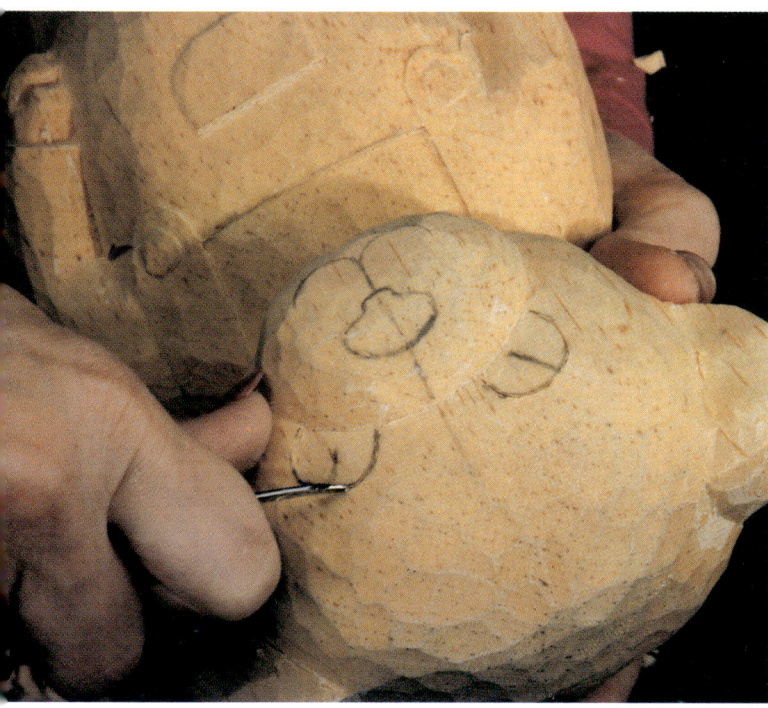

Score around the eyes.

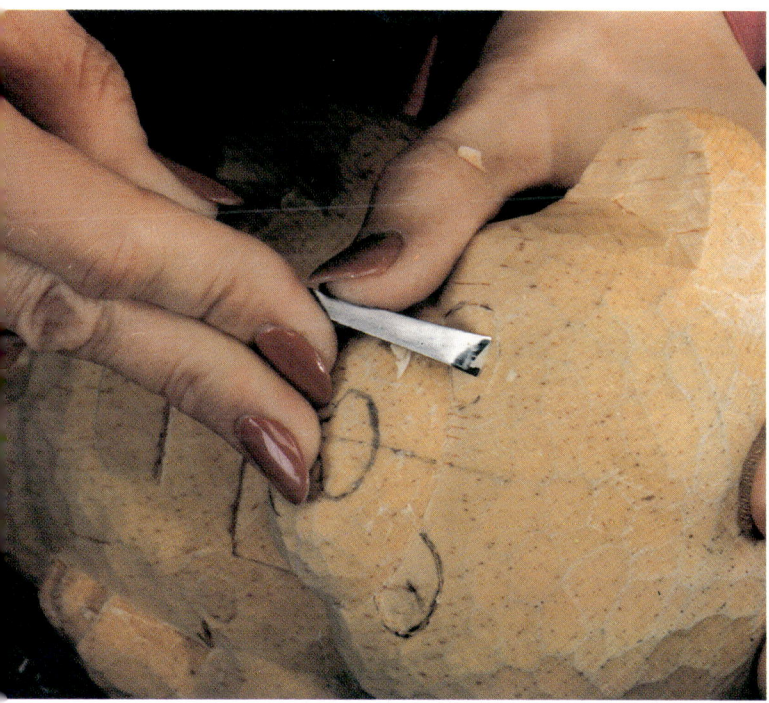

Round the eyes back to the score lines.

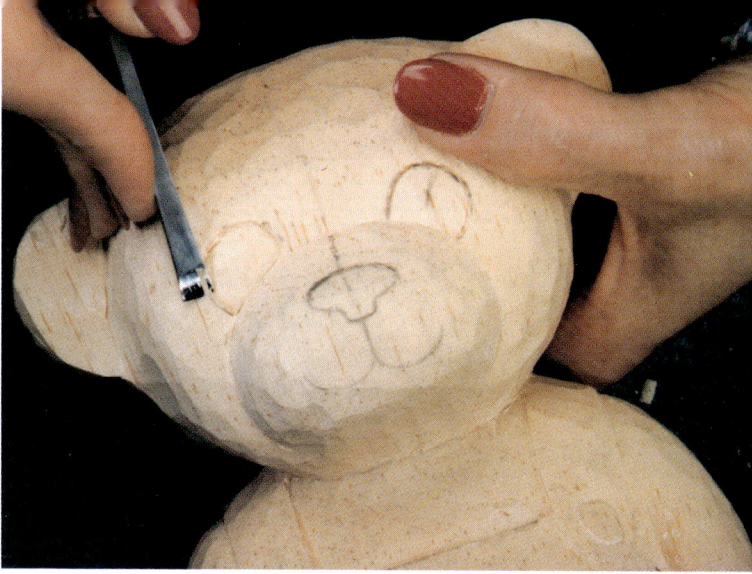

Round the outside edge around the eye.

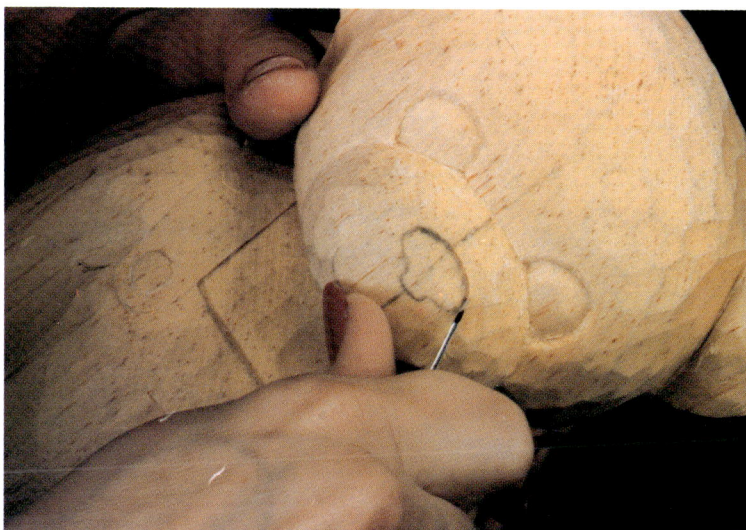

Score shallowly around the nose.

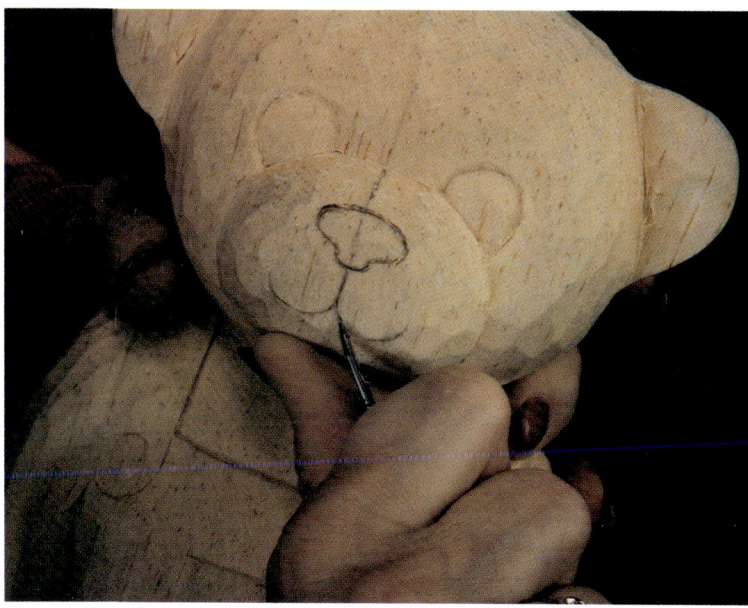

Continue on the lines of the mouth.

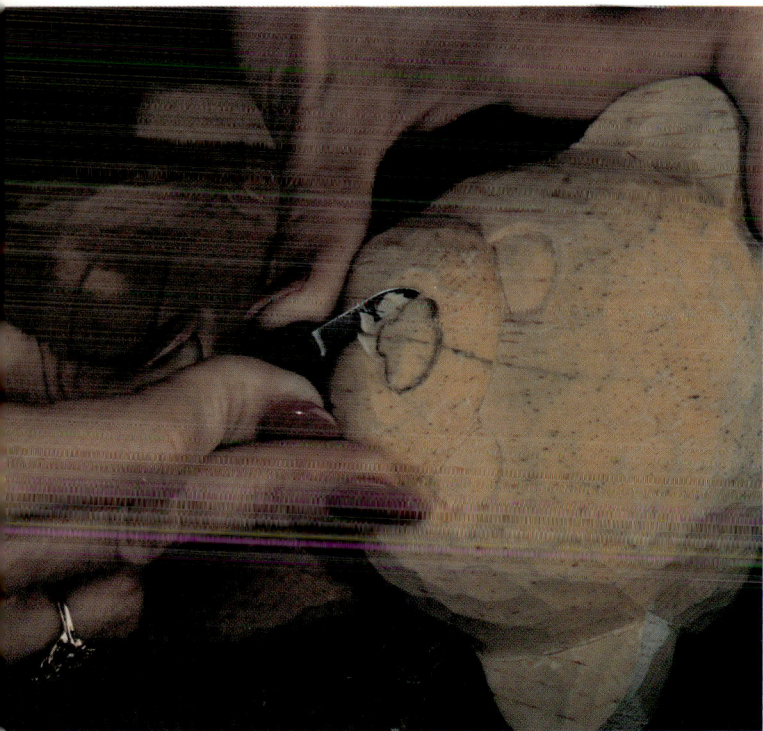

Relieve the muzzle around the nose.

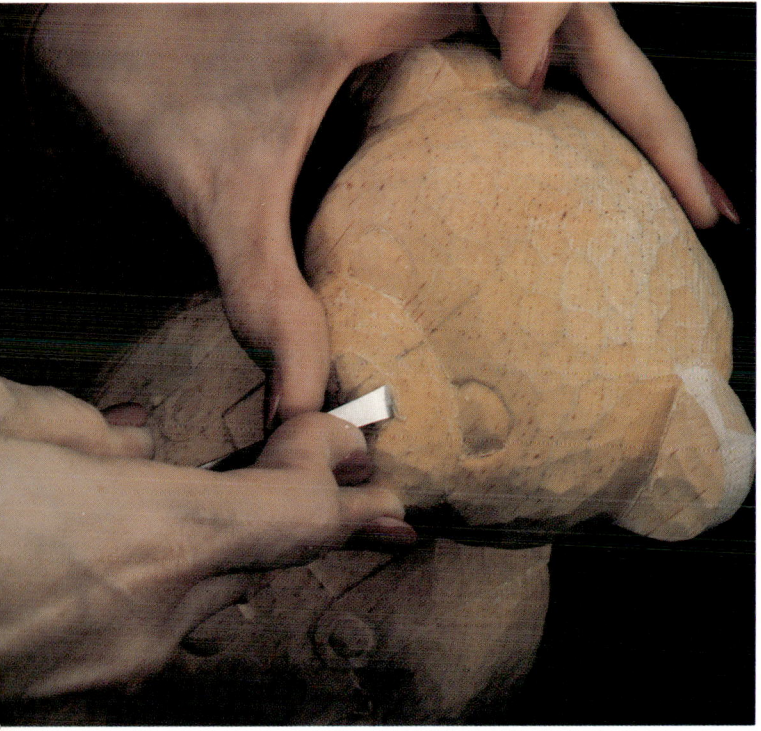

Round the nose back to the score line.

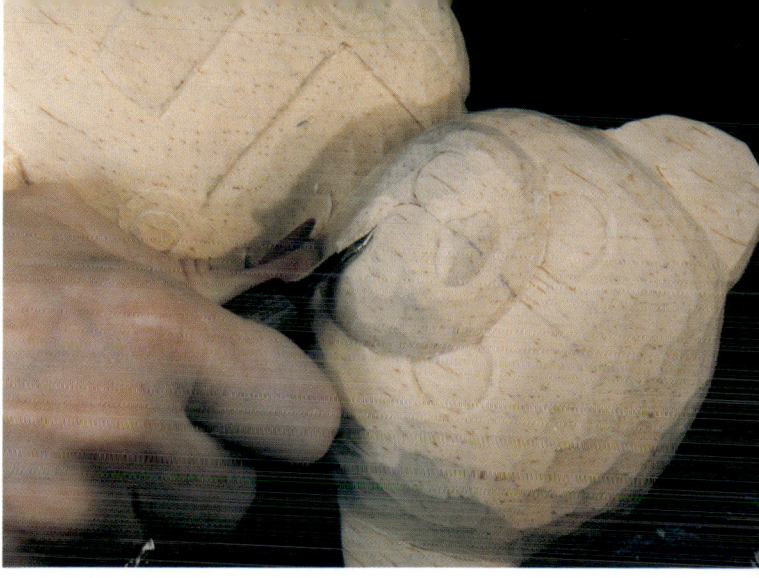

At the mouth, round the lip and drop the chin down.

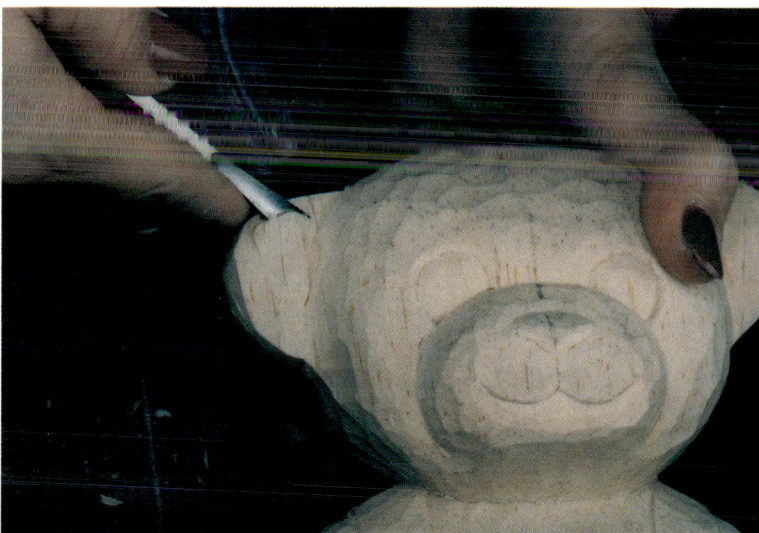

Cutting toward the head, scoop out the ear with a gouge. If you go from the head out, you are likely to chip the wood of the ear.

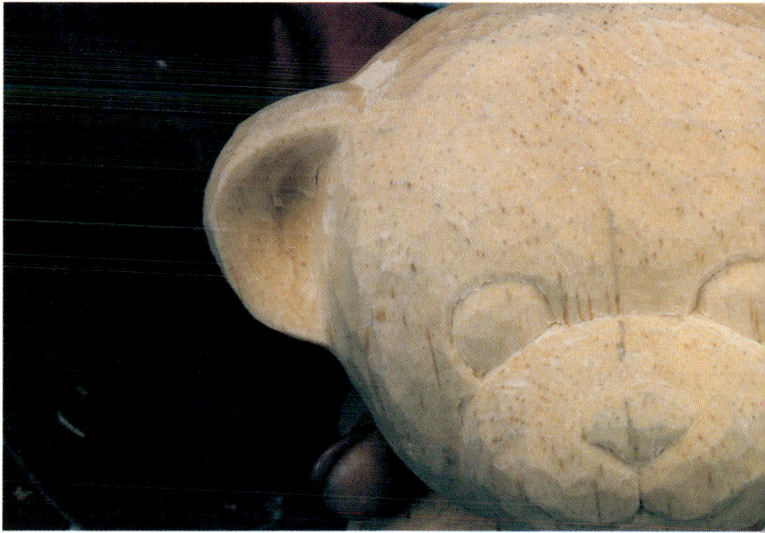

One ear complete.

34

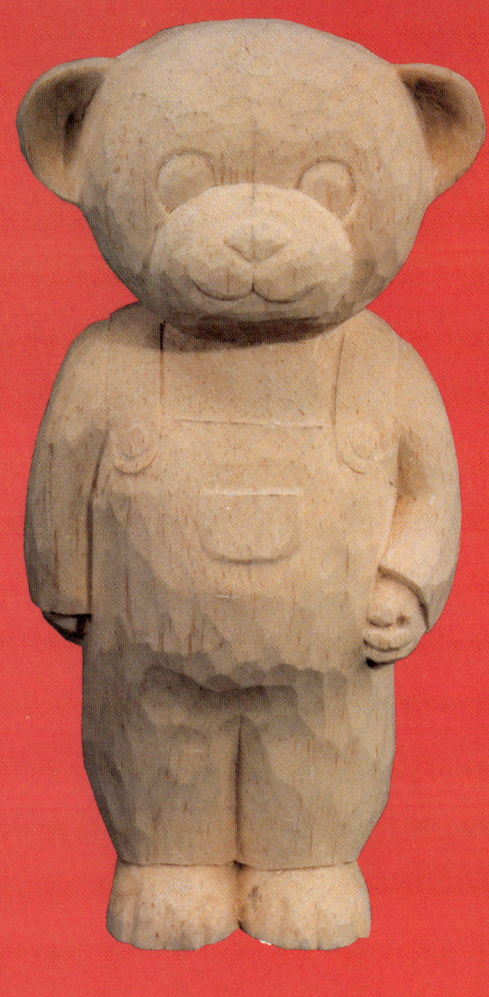
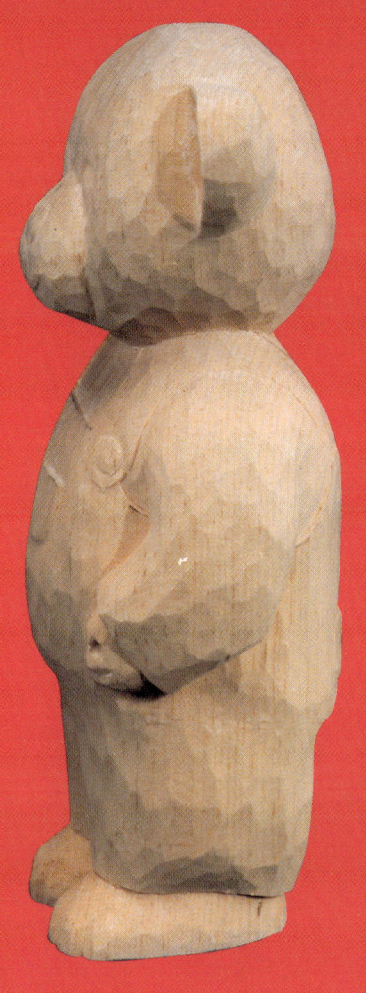
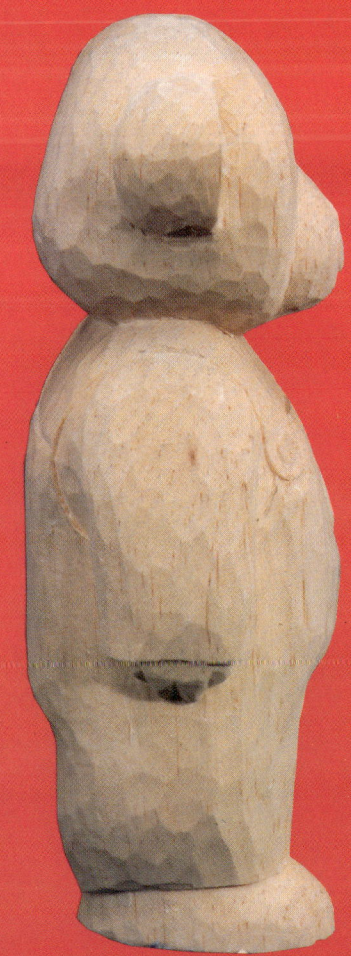
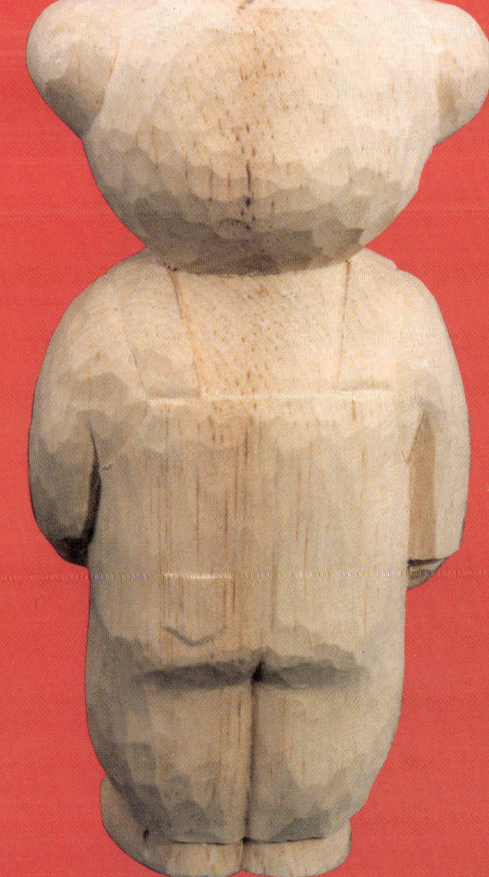

Ready for painting.

PAINTING THE TEDDY BEAR

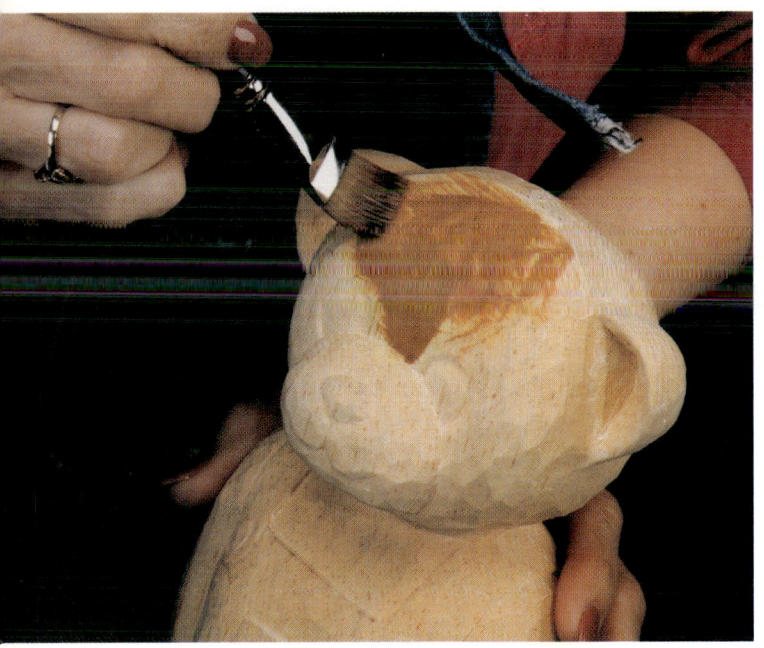

Base coat the fur areas with raw sienna.

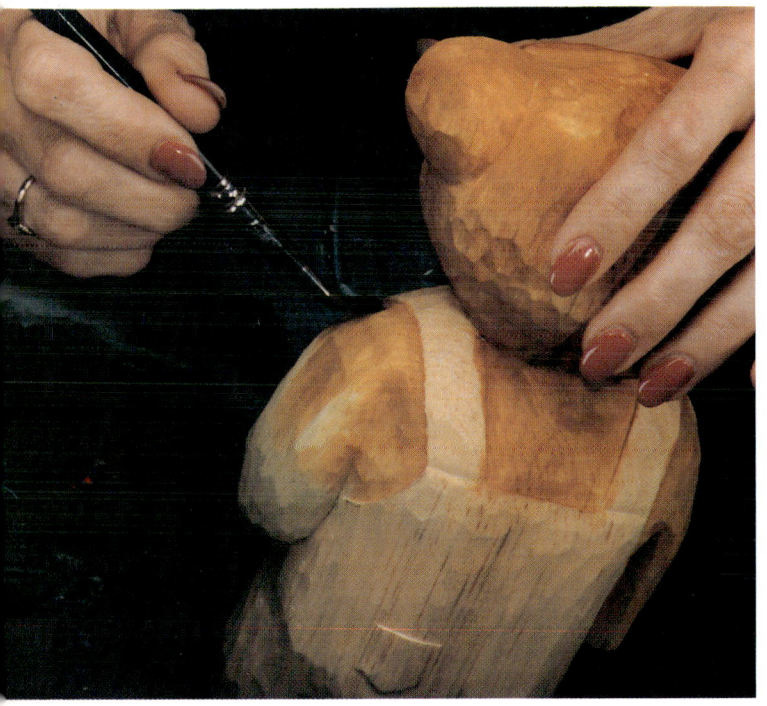

I also use the raw sienna to undercoat the shirt.

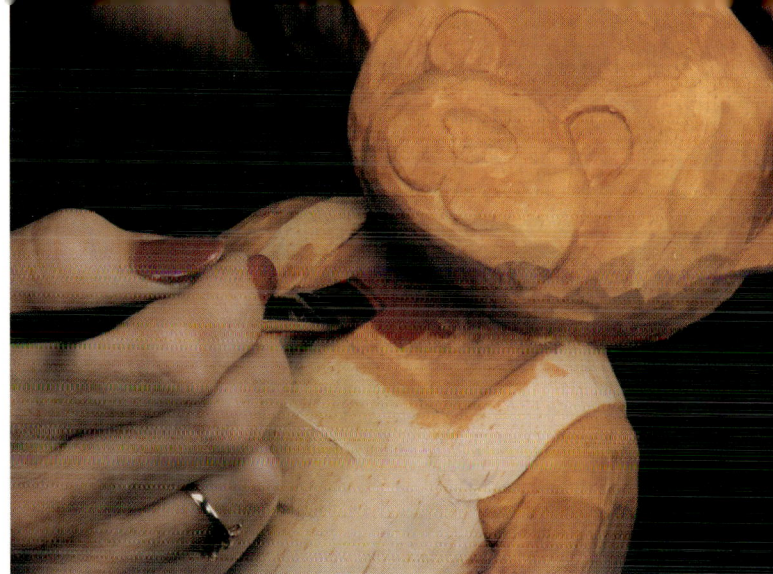

Apply red to the shirt, beginning with the chest...

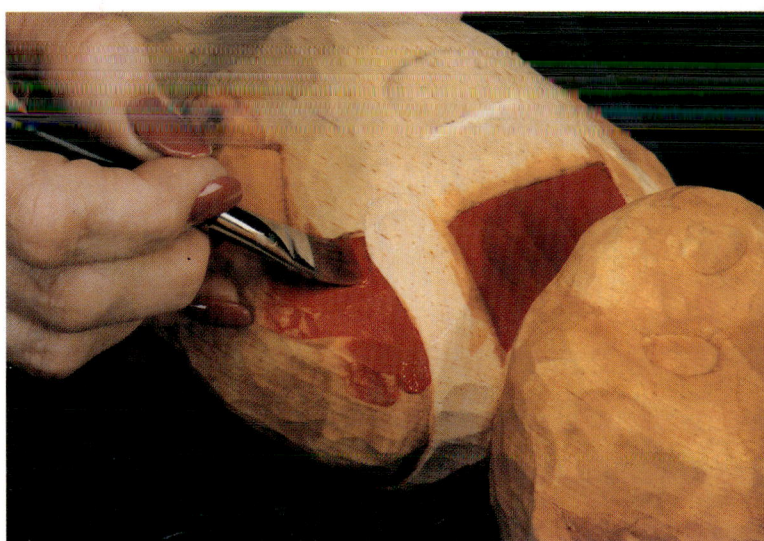

and continuing on the arms.

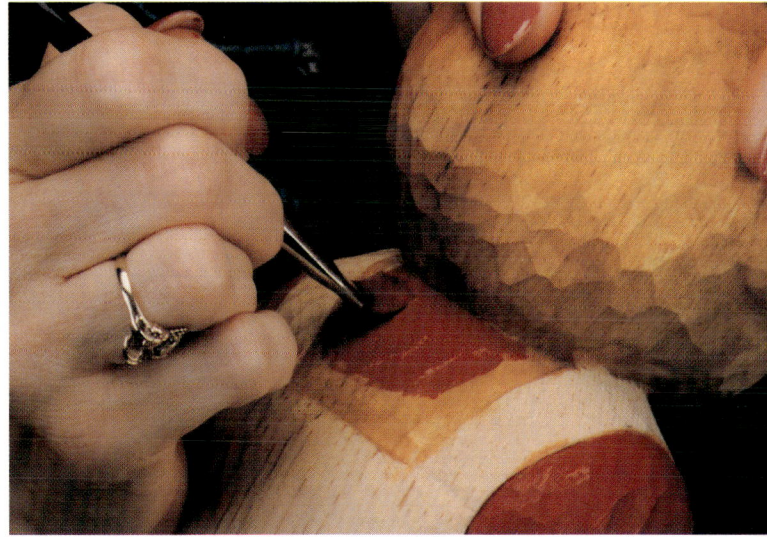

While I didn't need to be too careful with the raw sienna, I need to use more care with the red so it doesn't slop over too much.

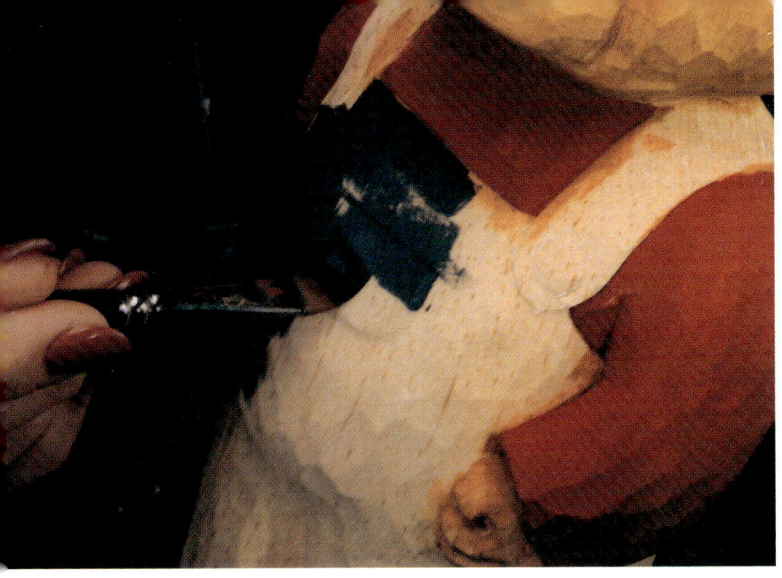

Apply blue to the overalls.

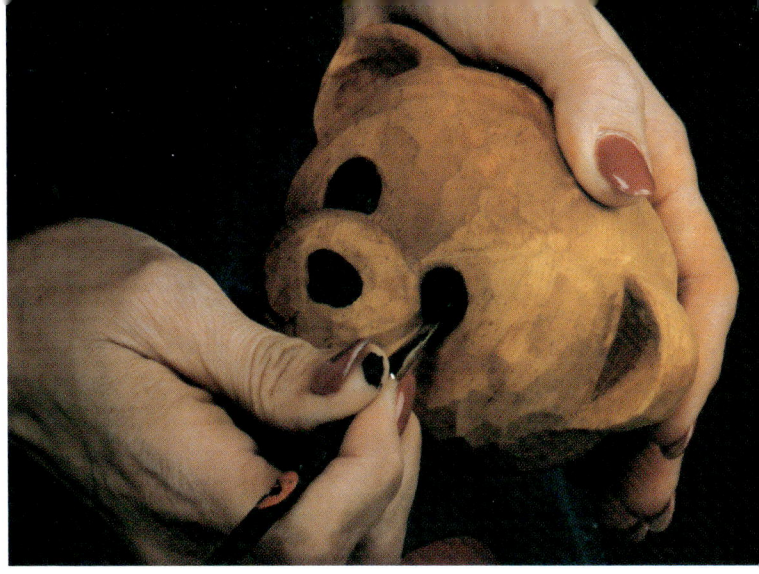

and the pupils of the eyes.

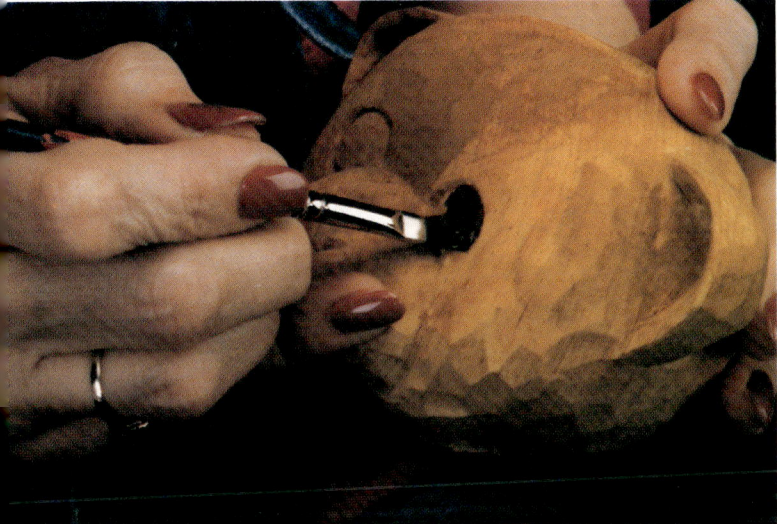

Paint the iris of the eye with burnt umber.

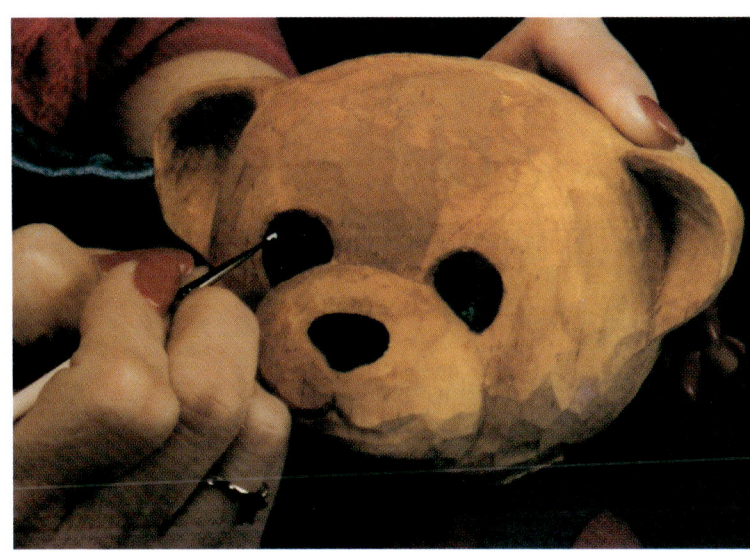

A white dot in one corner of the eye...

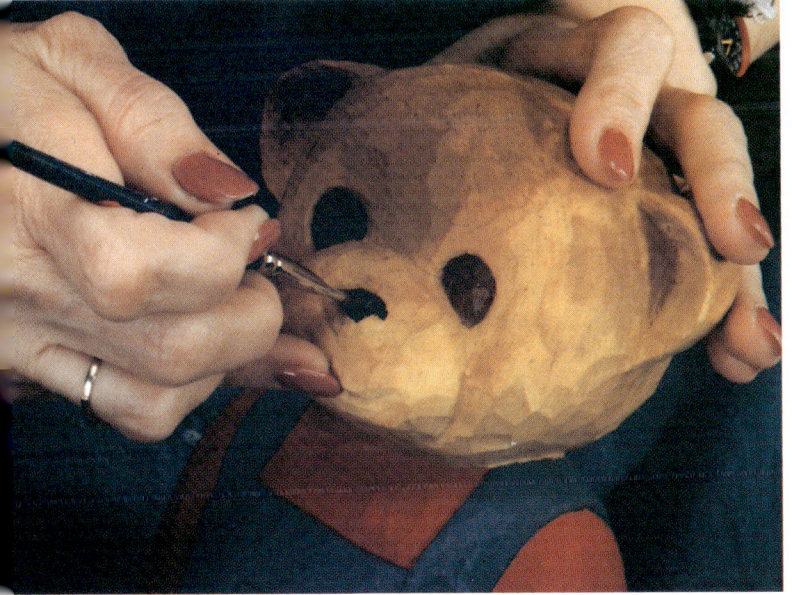

Black does the nose...

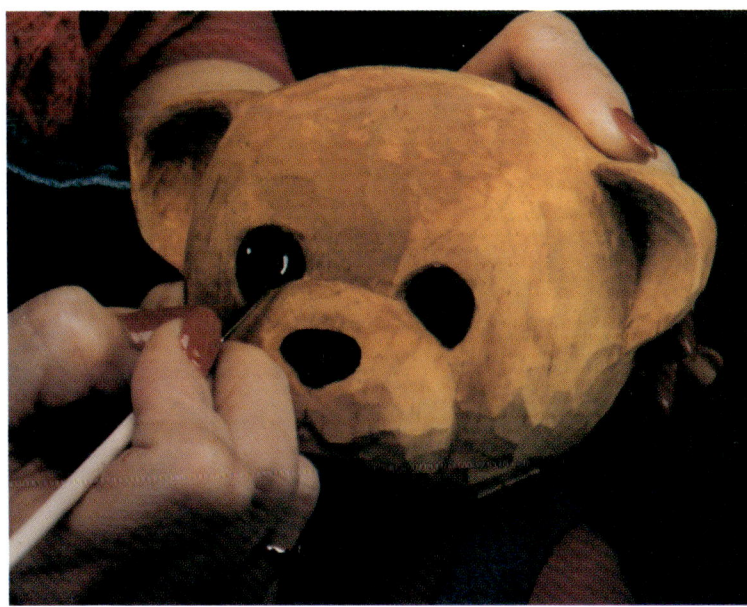

and a white line in the opposite corner give the eye life.

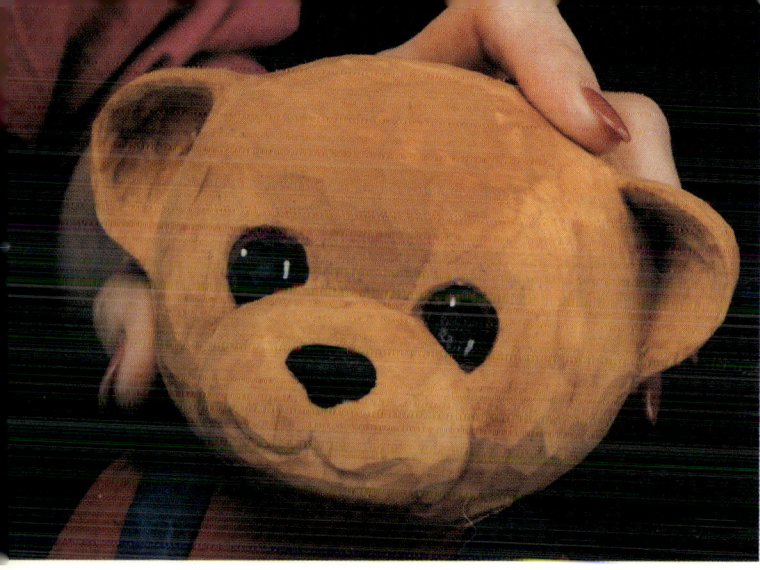

Both eyes should have the sparkle in the same position.

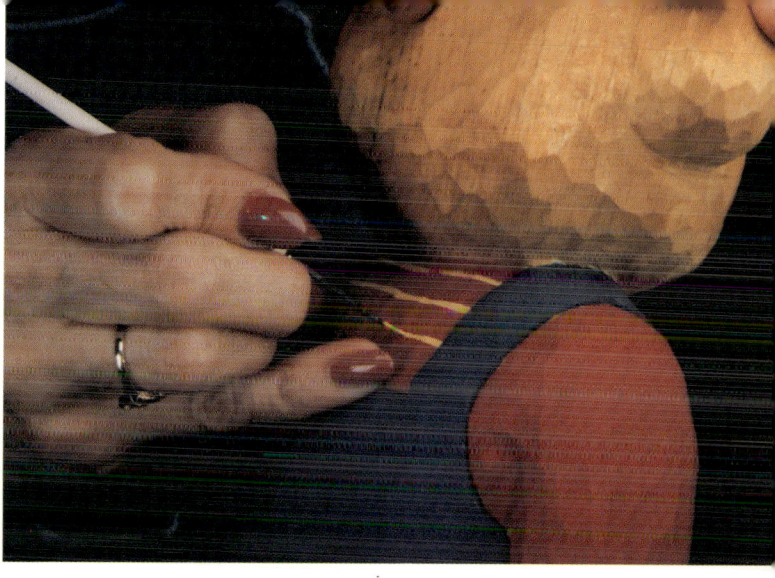

Use straw colored paint to add stripes to the shirt.

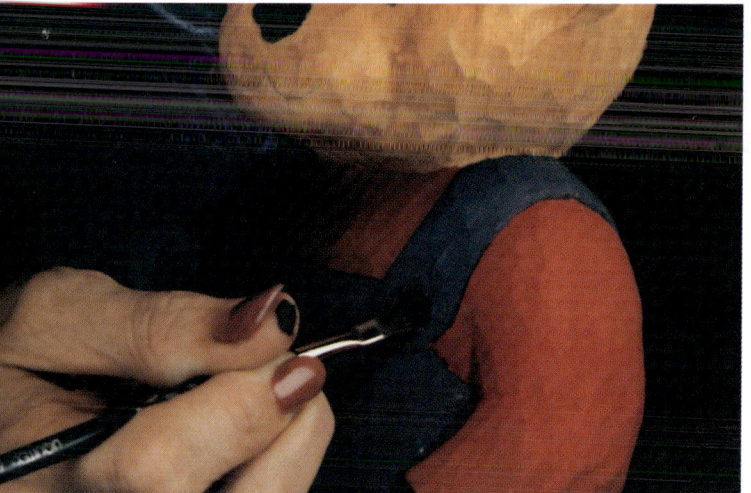

Paint the button of the overalls with burnt umber.

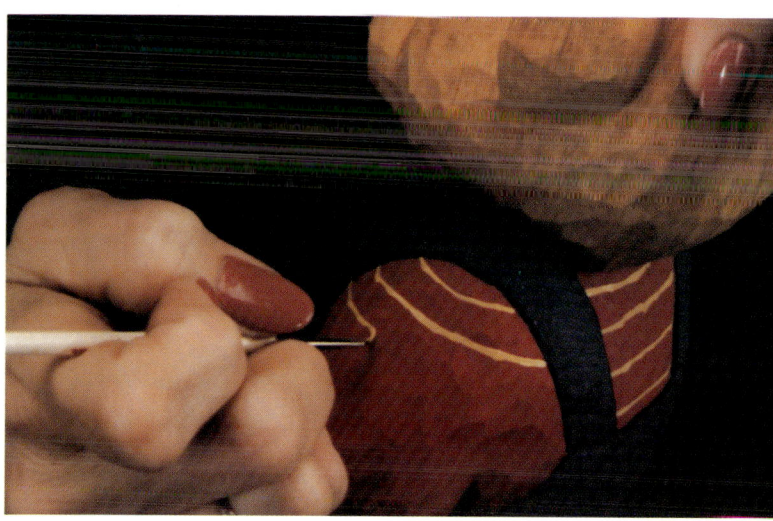

Continue the lines around the arms.

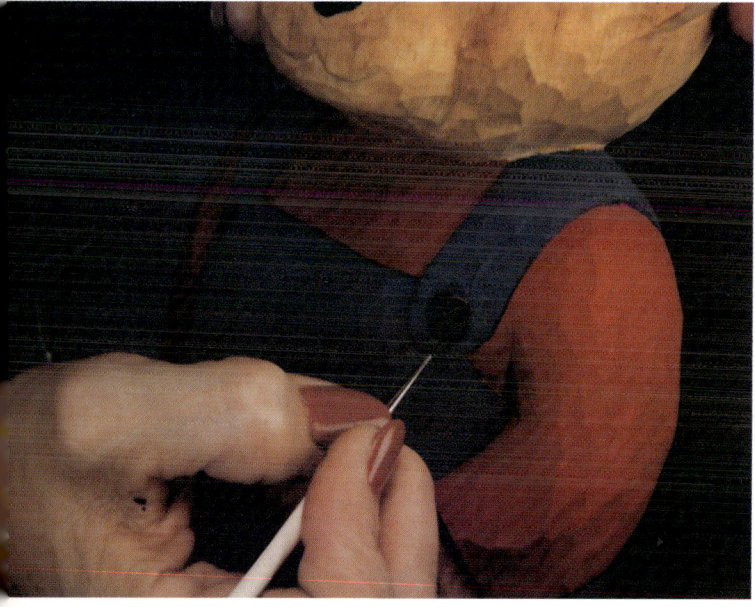

Add four button holes and crossed threads to the buttons with black paint.

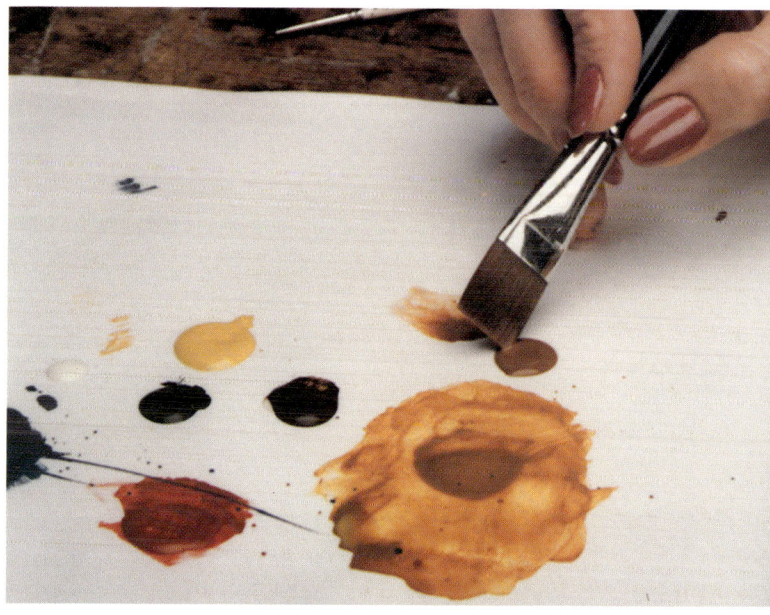

For shadowing corner load the brush with nutmeg, by dipping one corner in the paint...

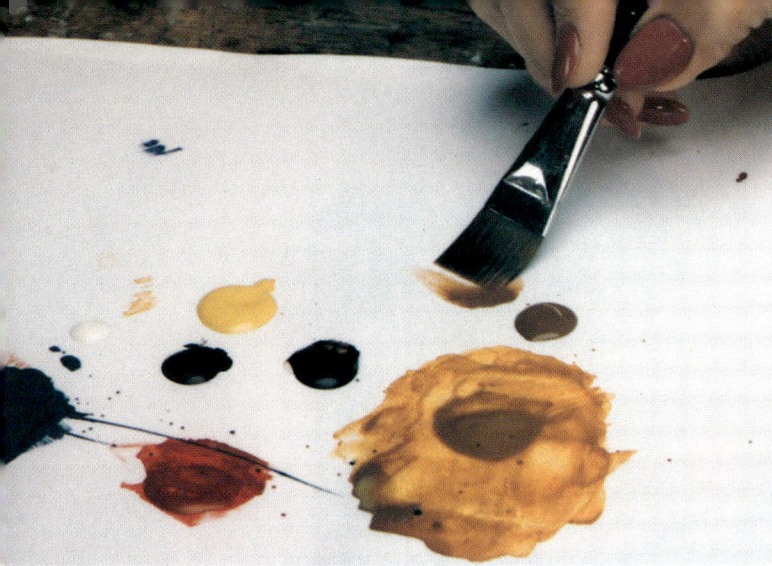

and working the paint into the bristles, creating a gradation of pigment from heavy at the corner to light.

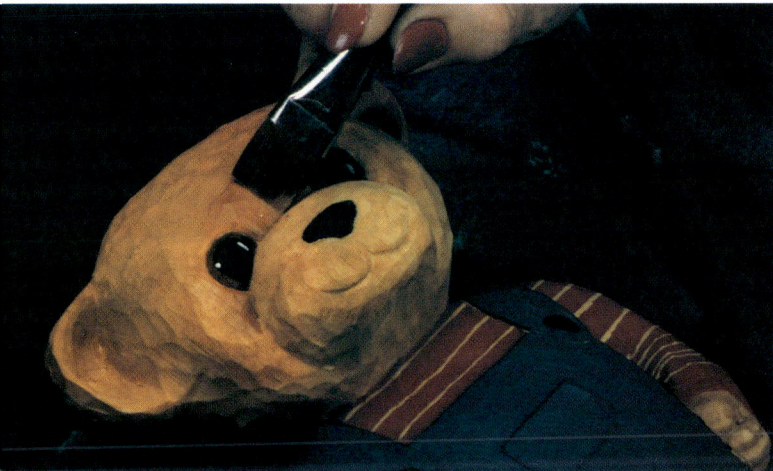

With the heavy side down toward the muzzle, add a shadow at the eye.

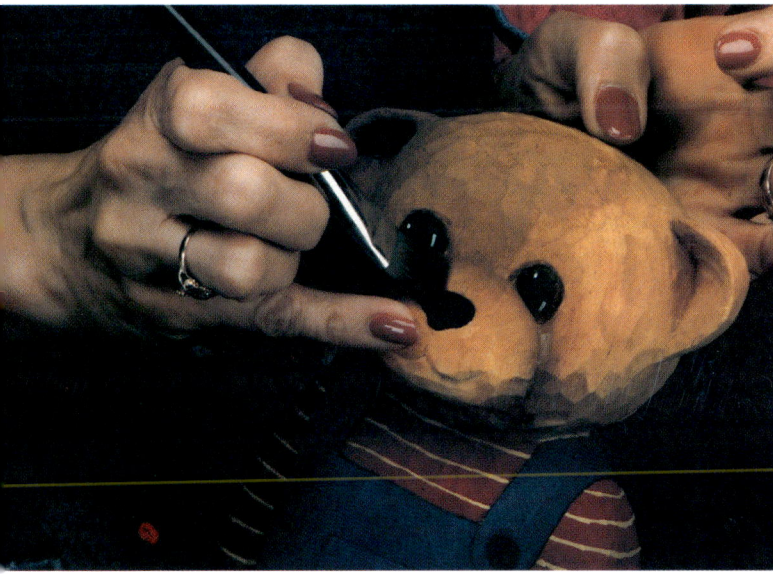

In a similar way come across the top of the muzzle with the heavily loaded area toward the eyes.

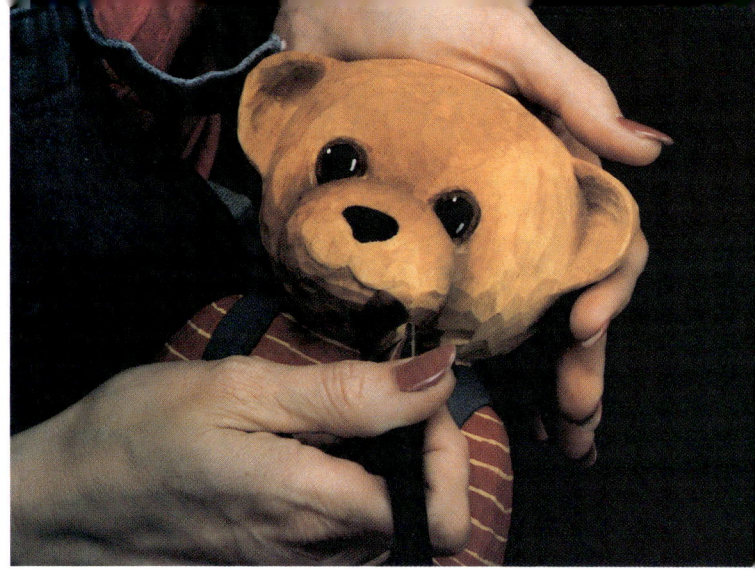

Run a shadow under the lips.

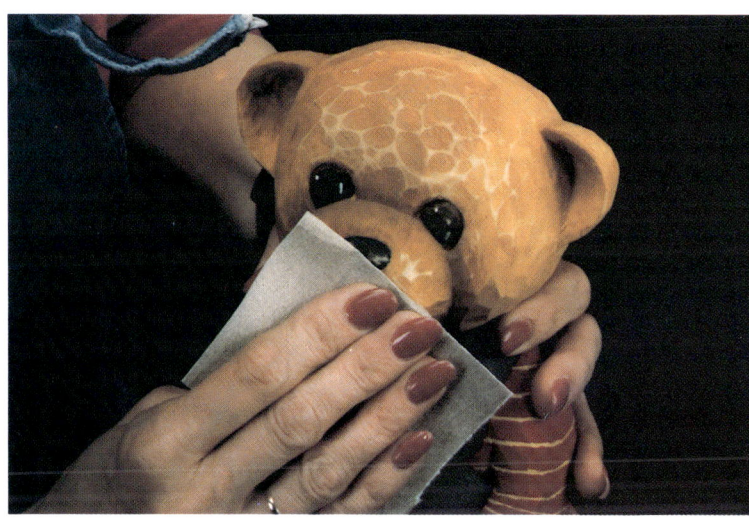

Lightly sand to hit the high spots, even on the eyes.

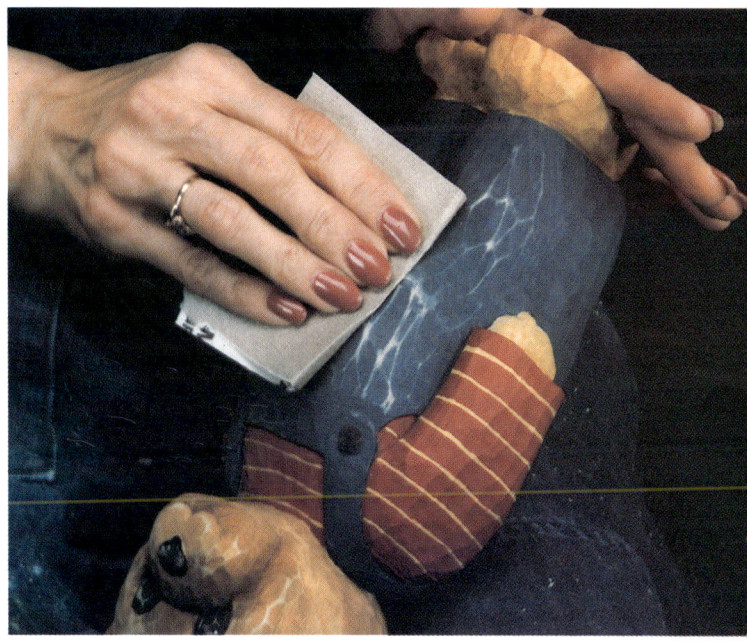

Continue with the clothing.

Load a brush with black paint.

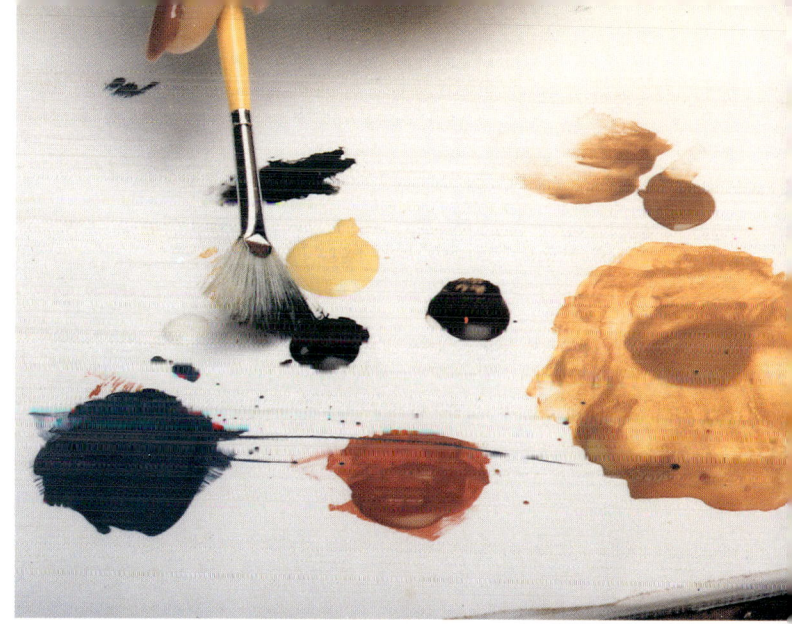

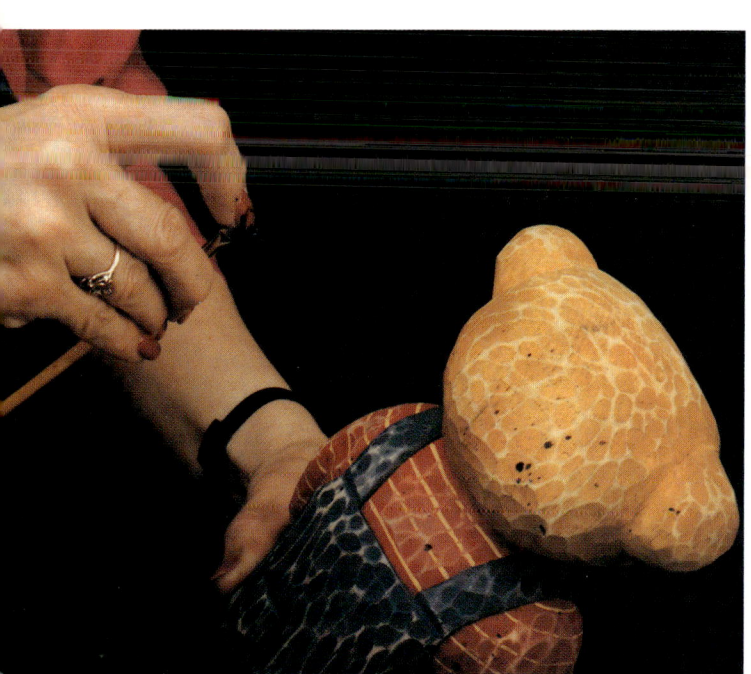

Use a finger to splatter the paint on the Teddy bear.

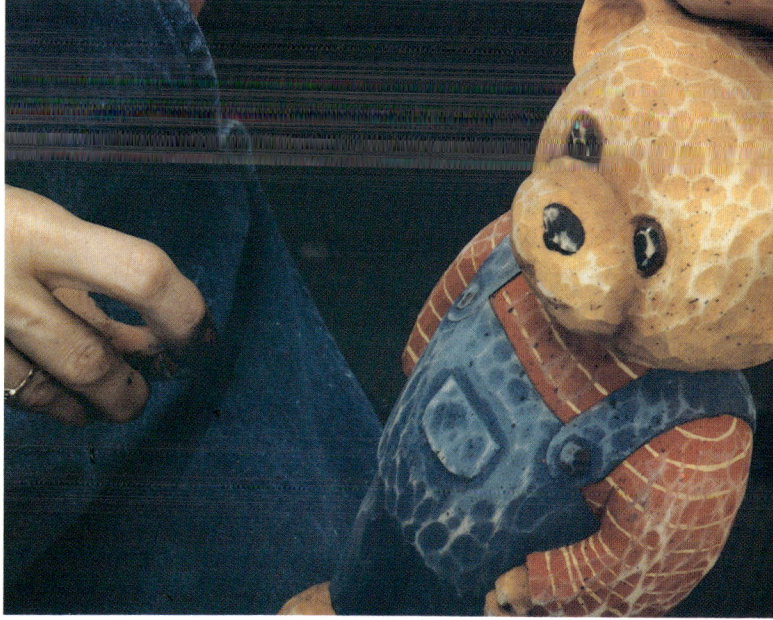

You may need to experiment until you find the right brush. An old toothbrush sometimes works very well.

You want a fine dotted effect.

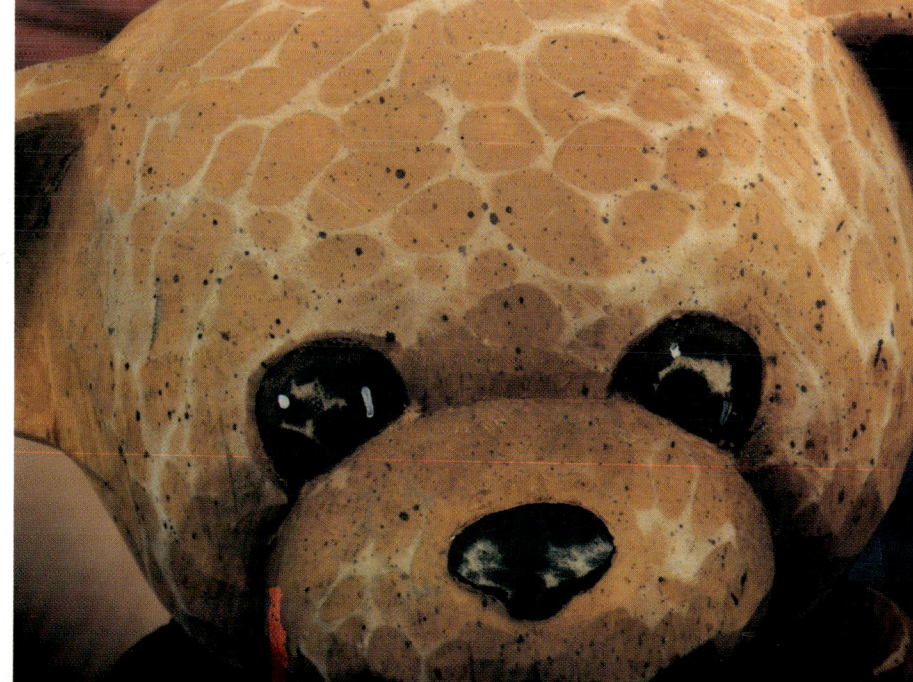

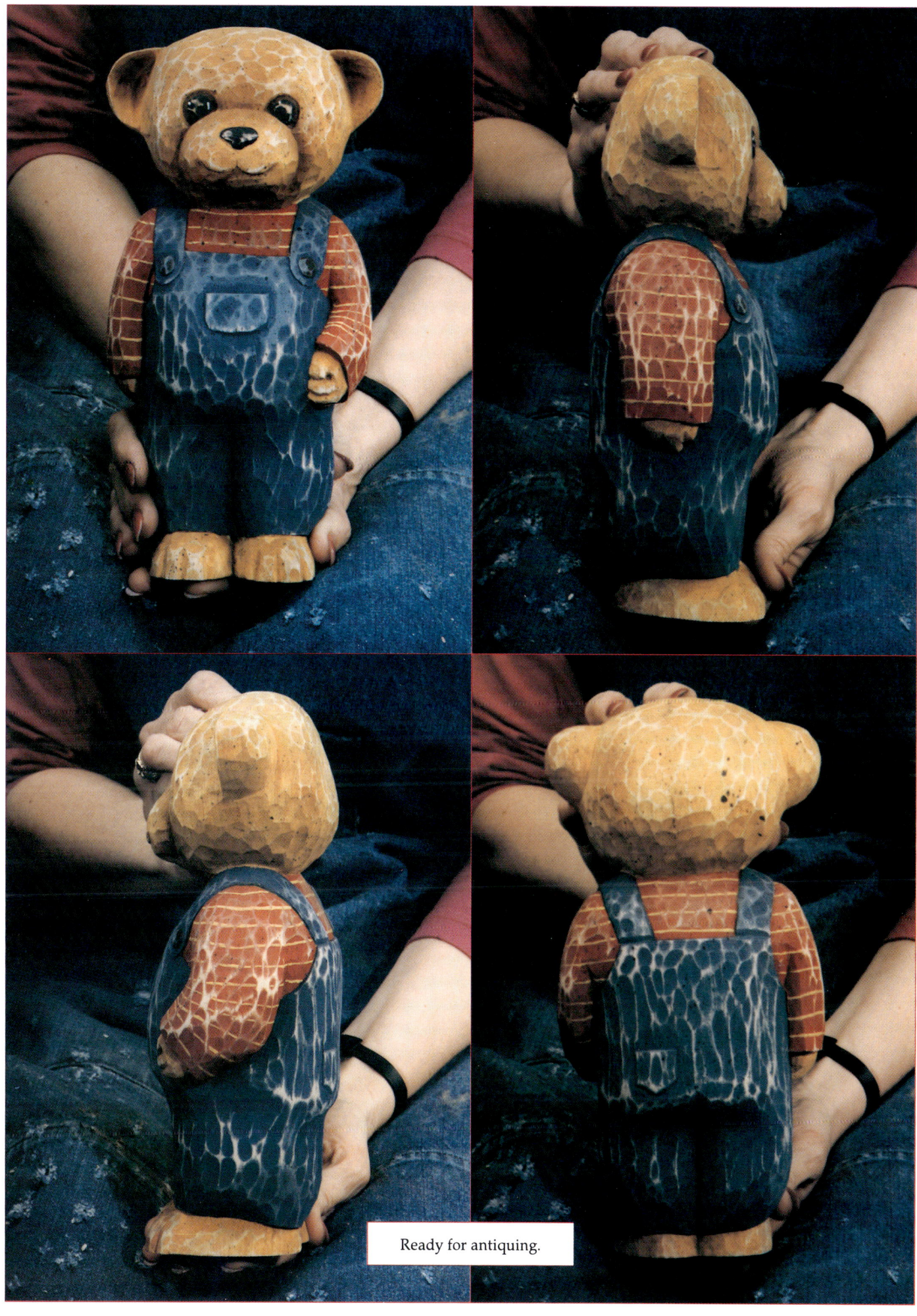

Ready for antiquing.

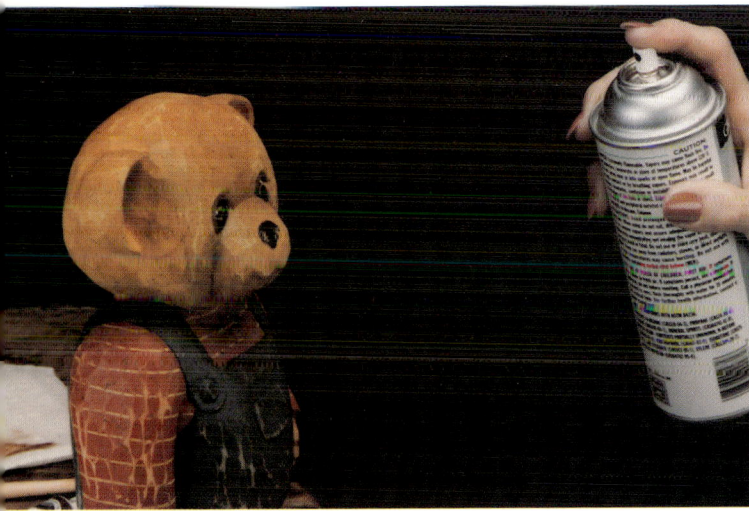

Apply at least 4 coats of fast drying varnish to the teddy.

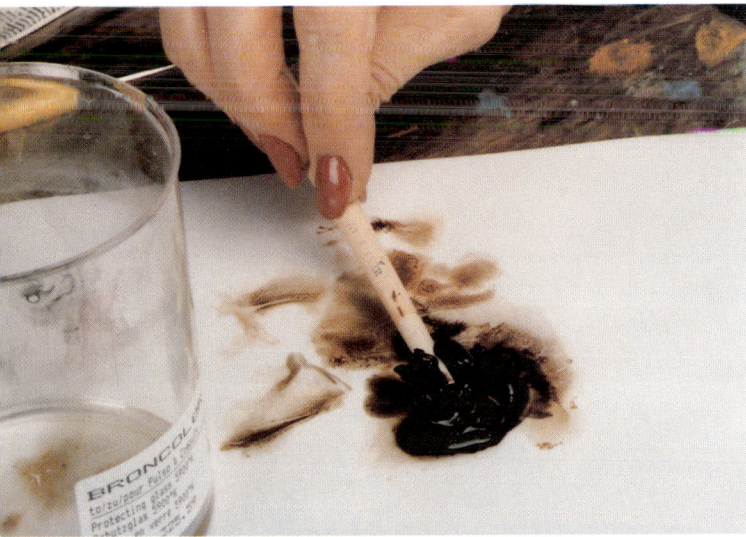

When it has thoroughly dried paint the entire figure with a coat of burnt umber artist's oils, thinned to the consistency of melted chocolate chips.

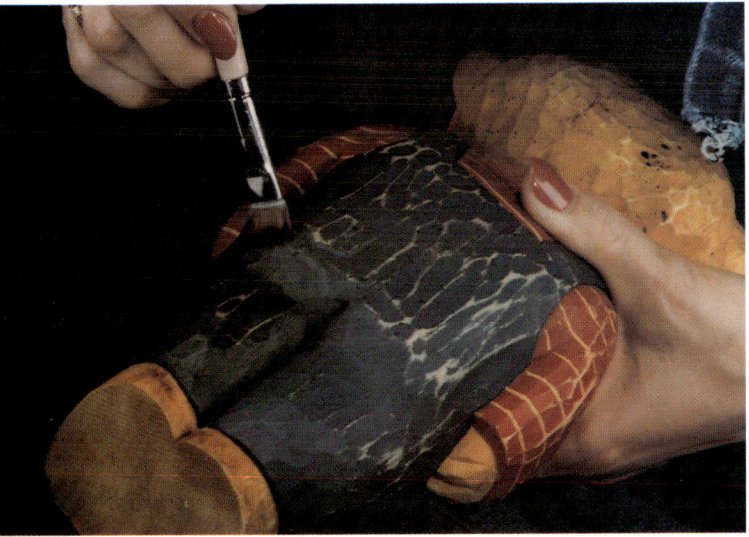

You should test it for compatibility in a small area first.

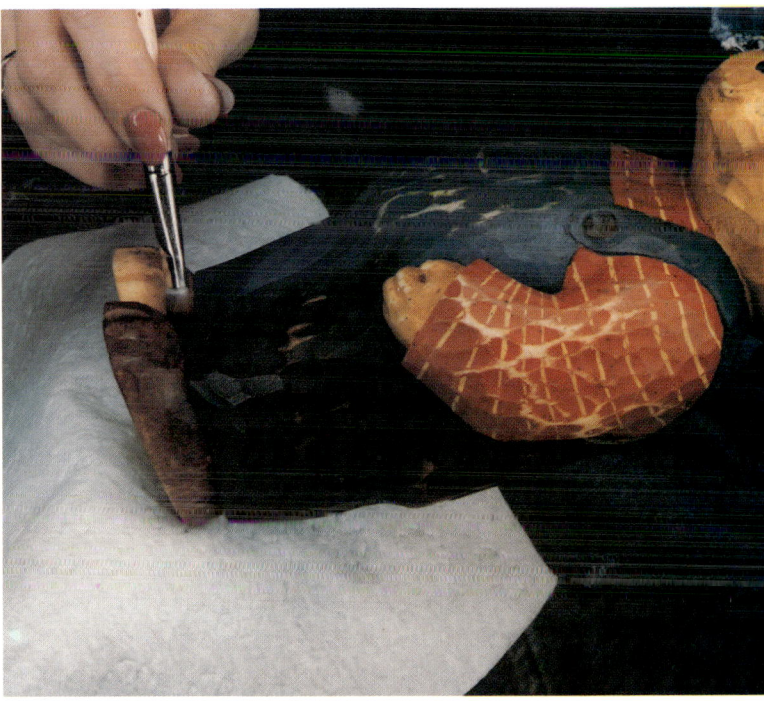

If things are all right continue painting the entire piece with the mixture.

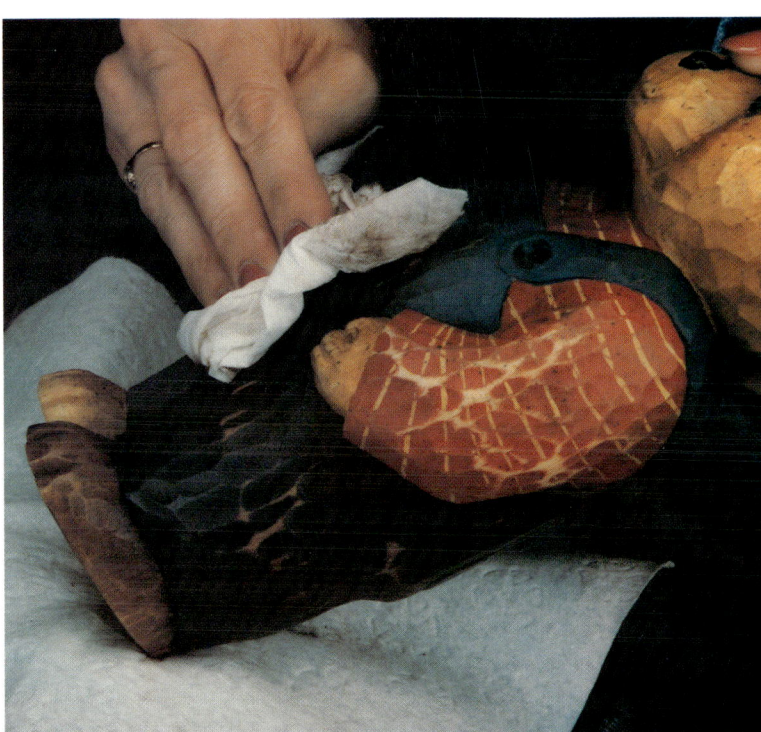

You may rub the piece down as you finish a section as I am here, or cover the whole piece before rubbing.

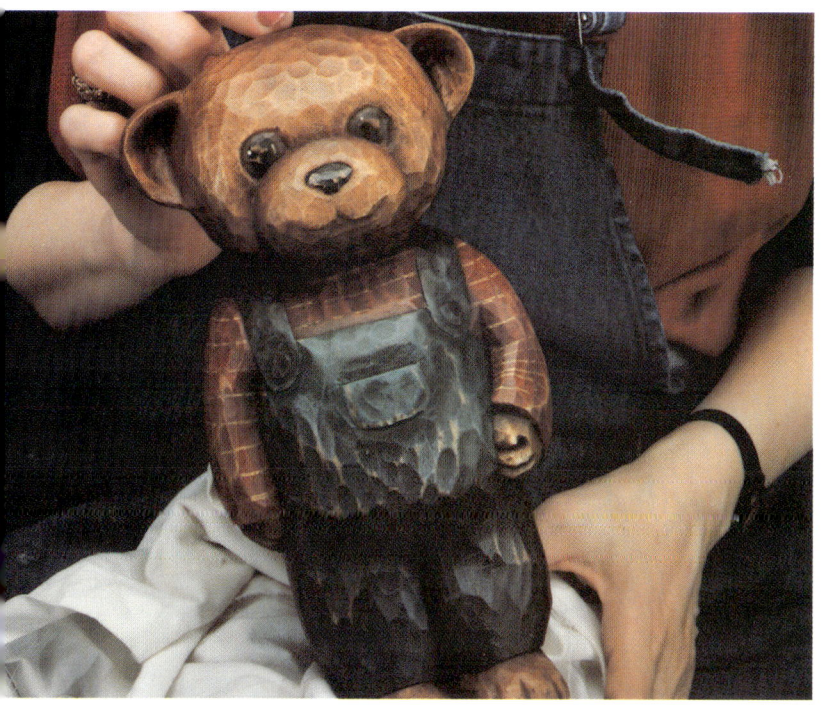

The final rub down complete.

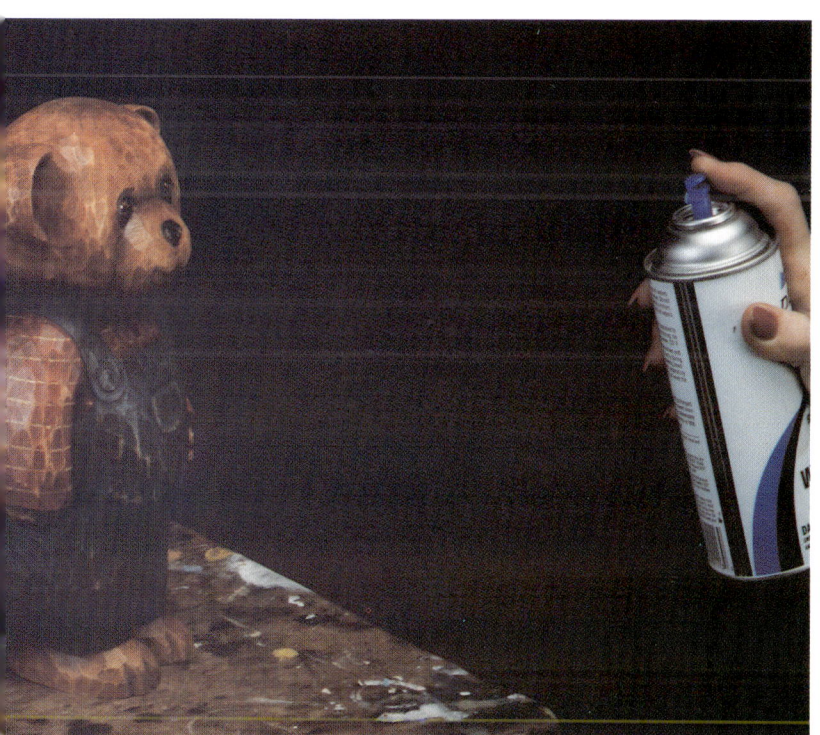

Allow the paint to dry for 48 hours, then spray with a light coat of wood finish.

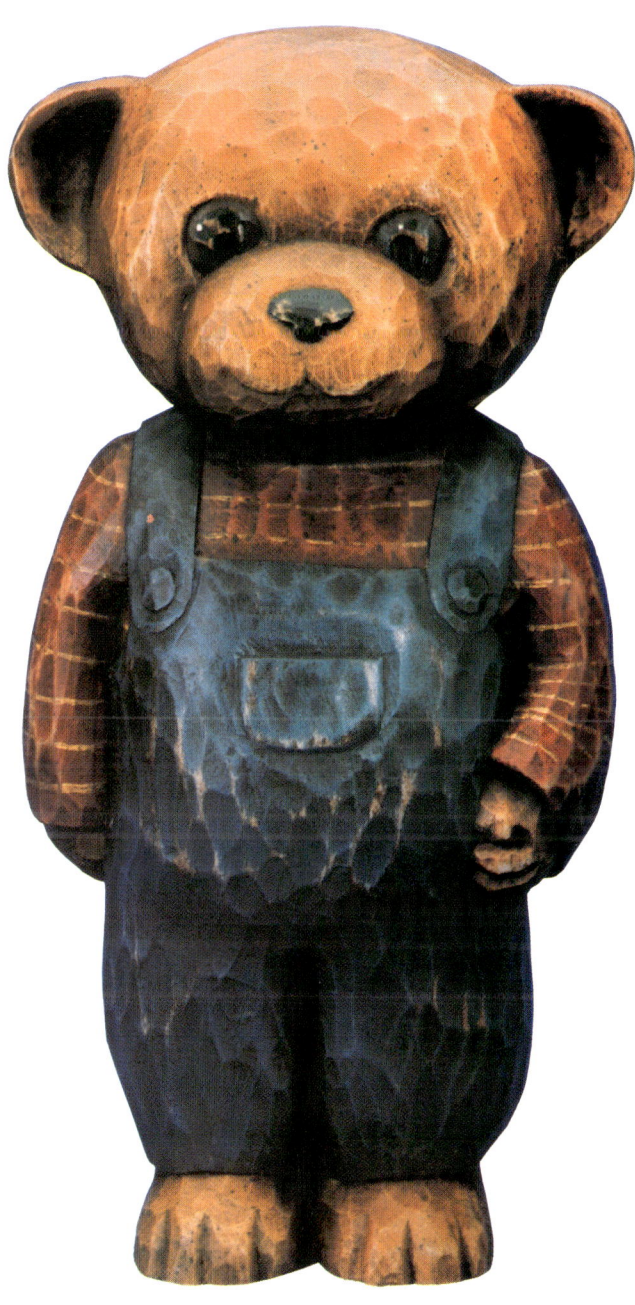

THE GALLERY AND PATTERNS

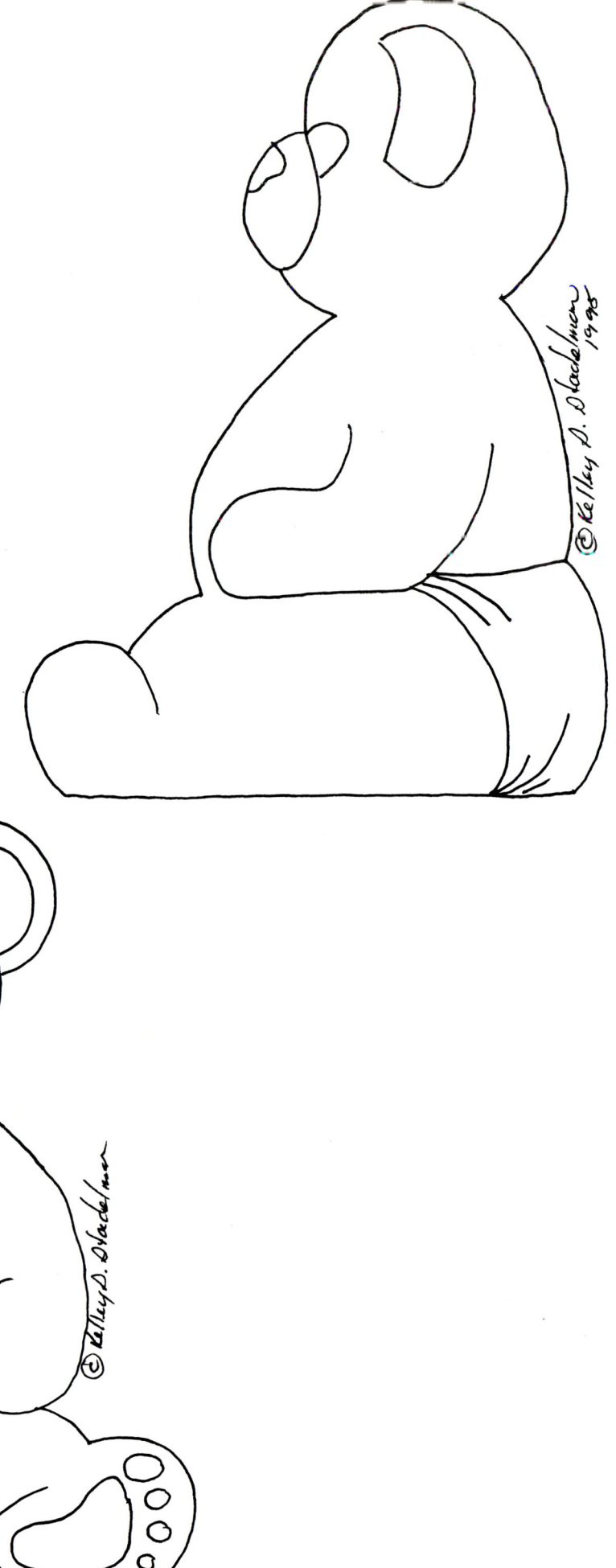

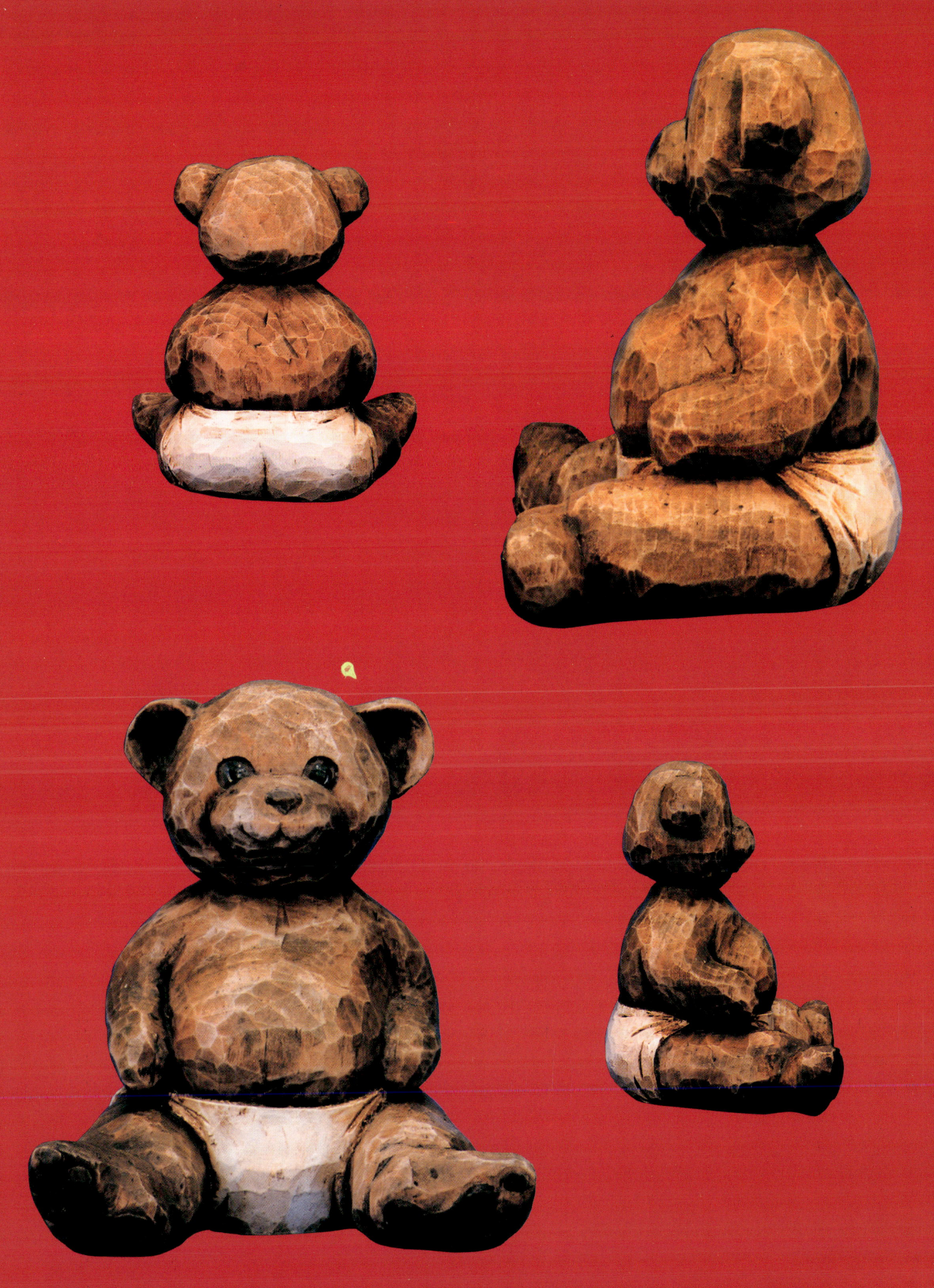

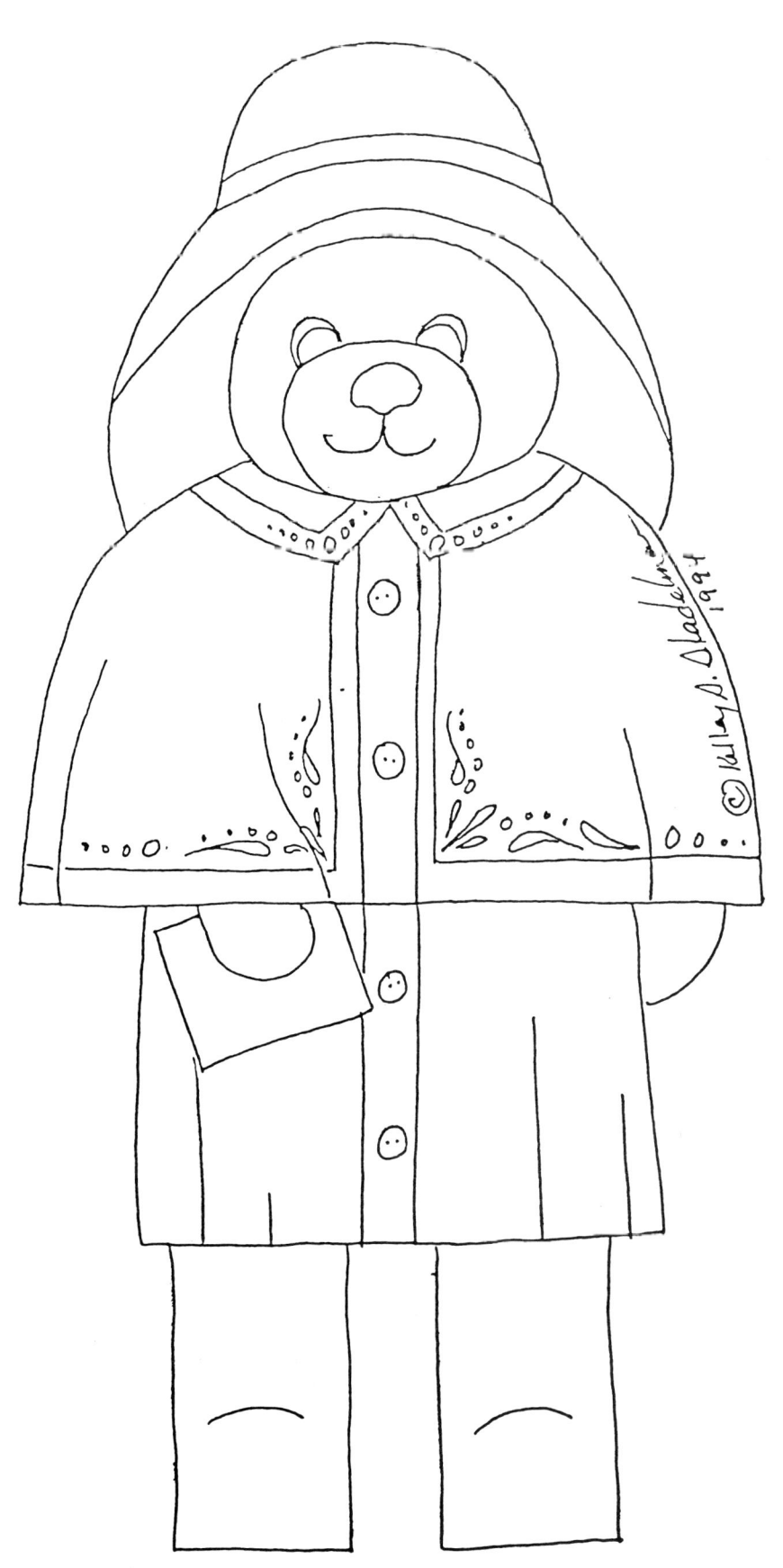

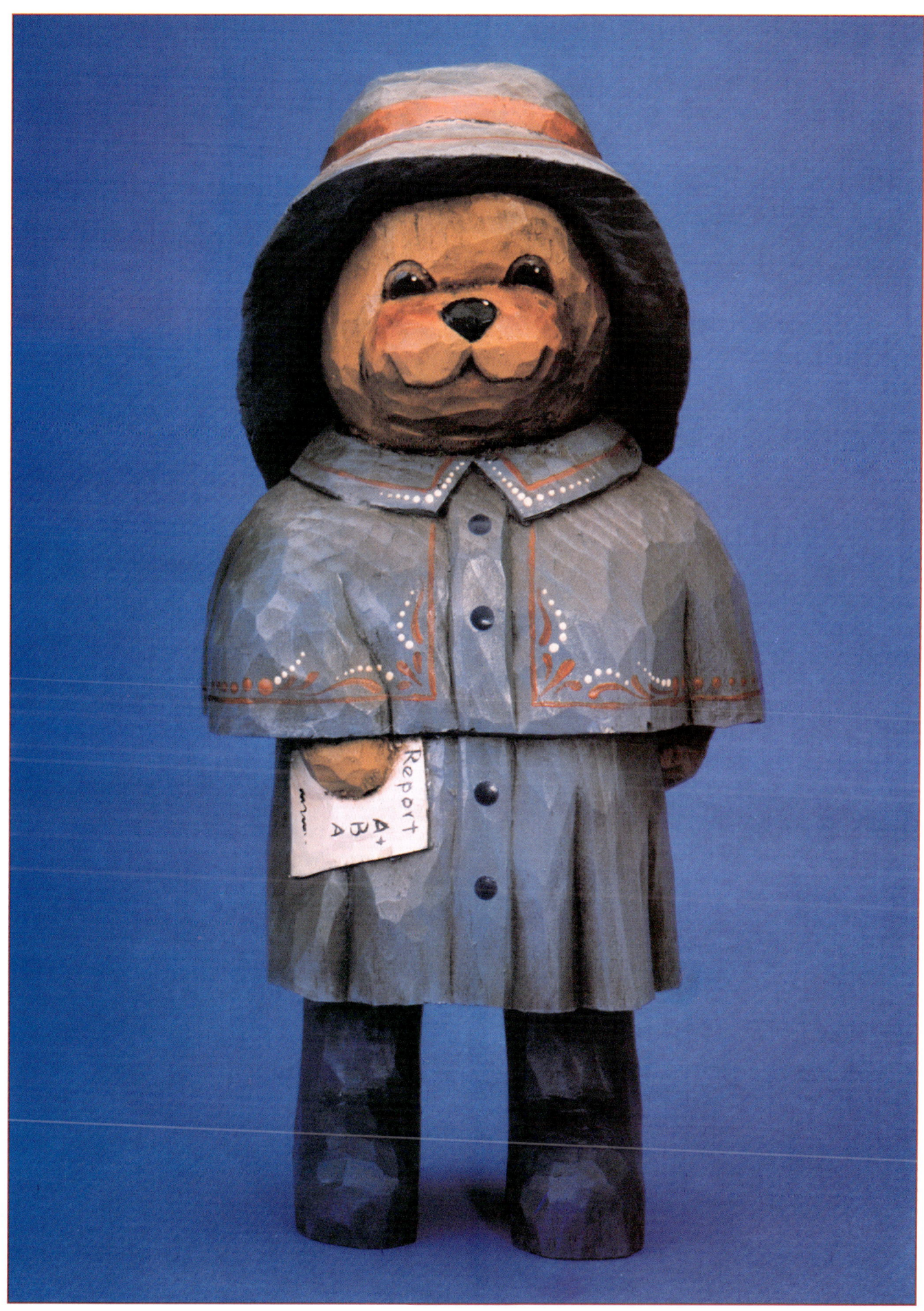

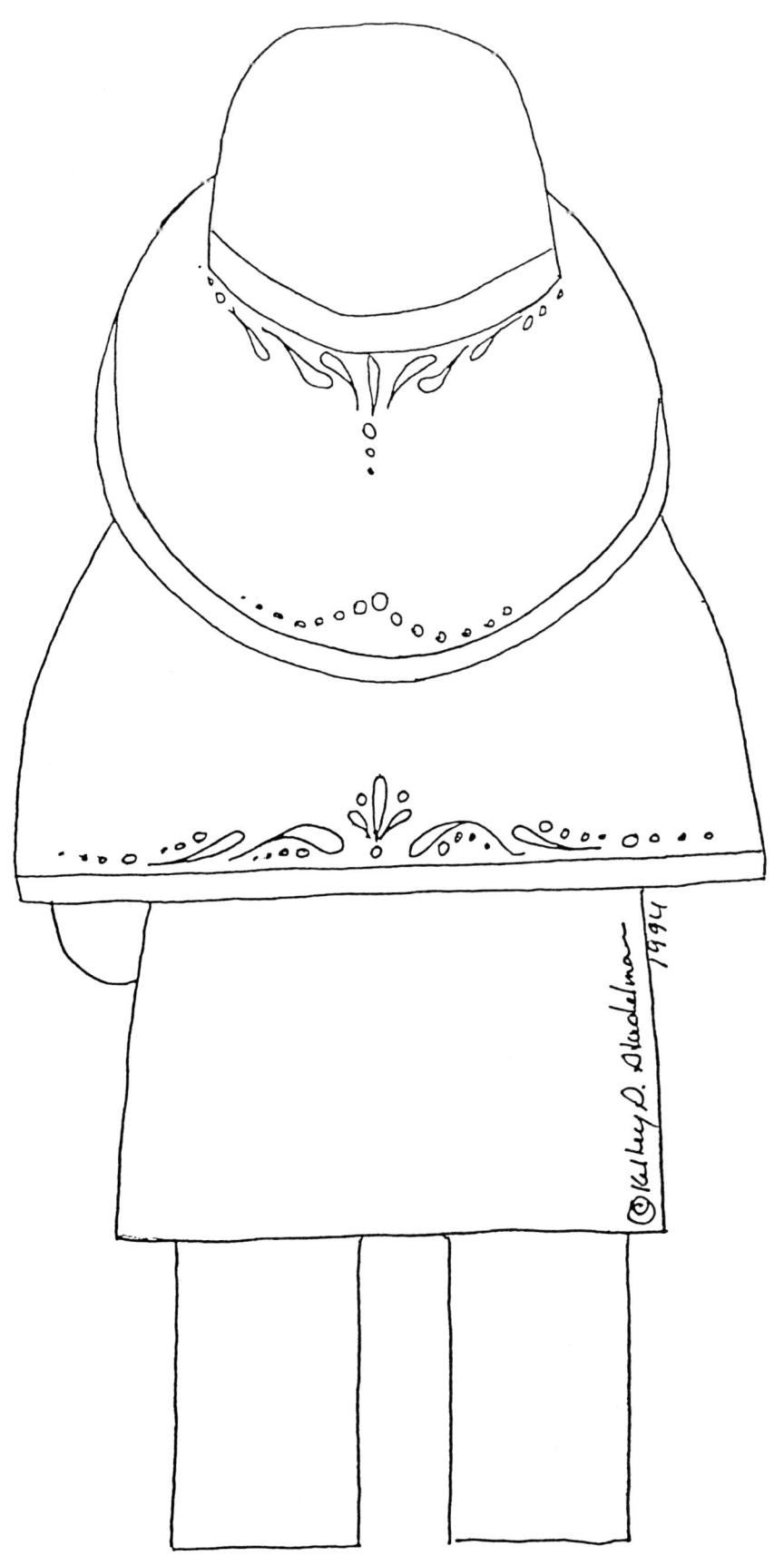

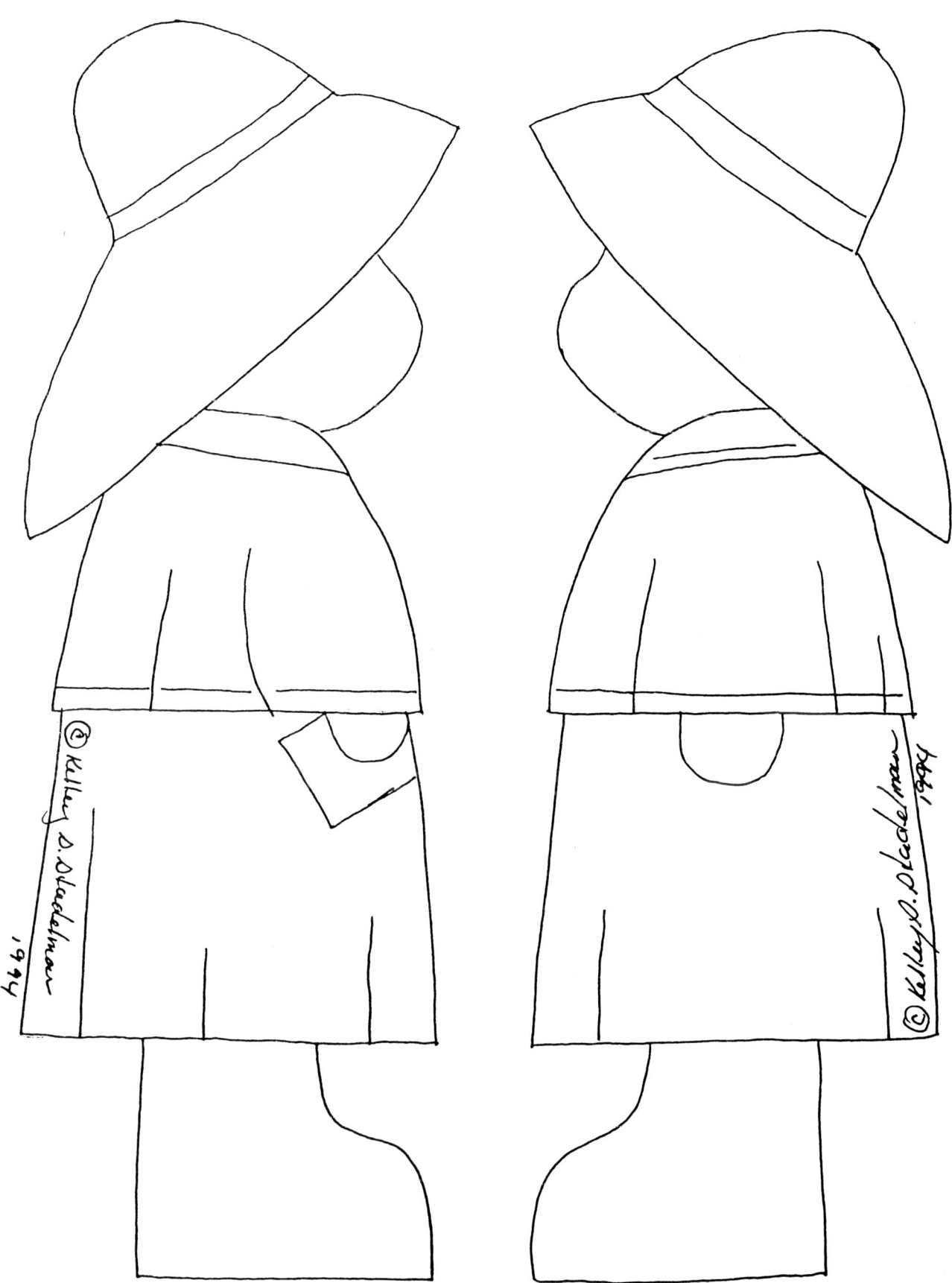

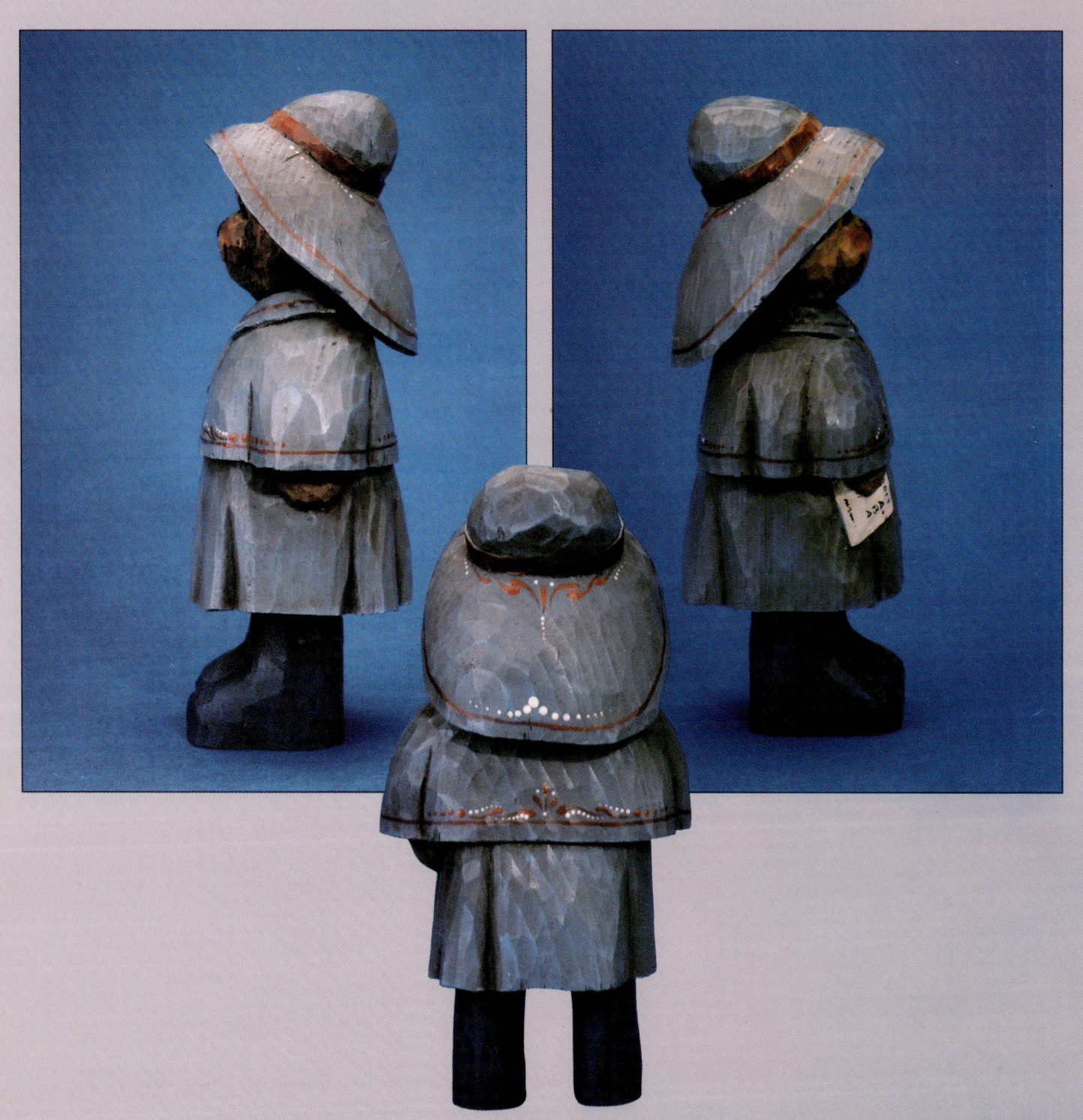

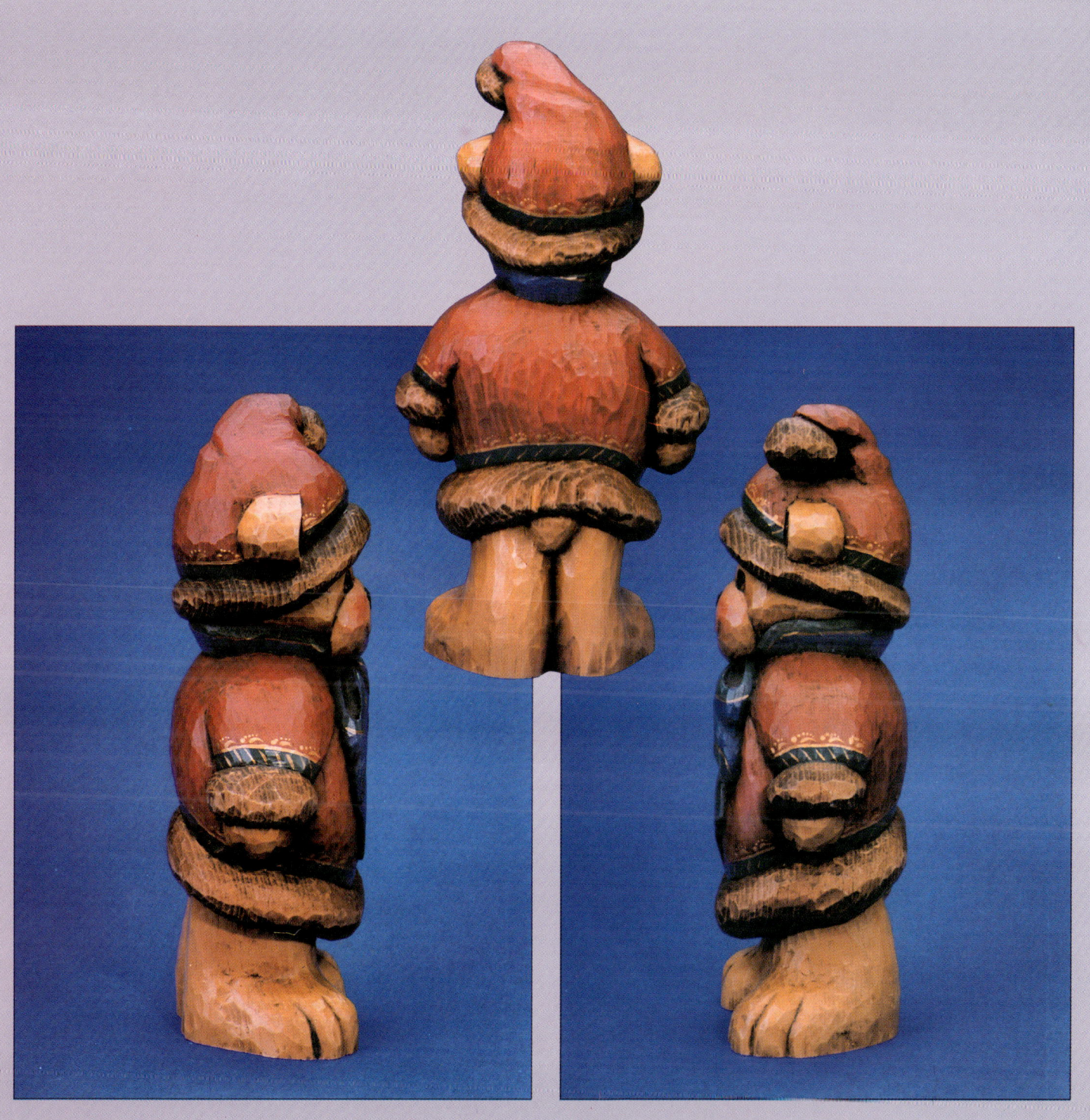

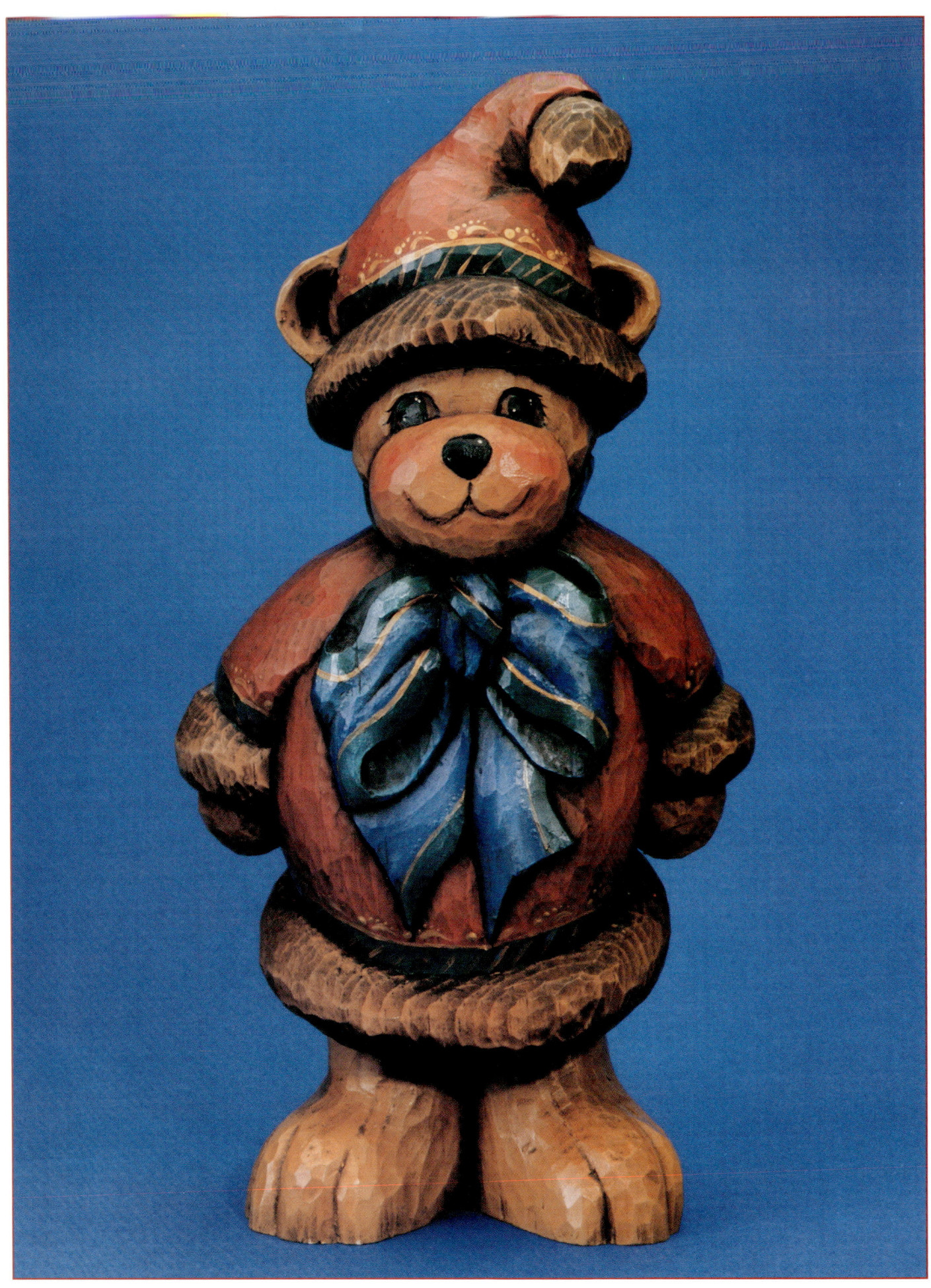

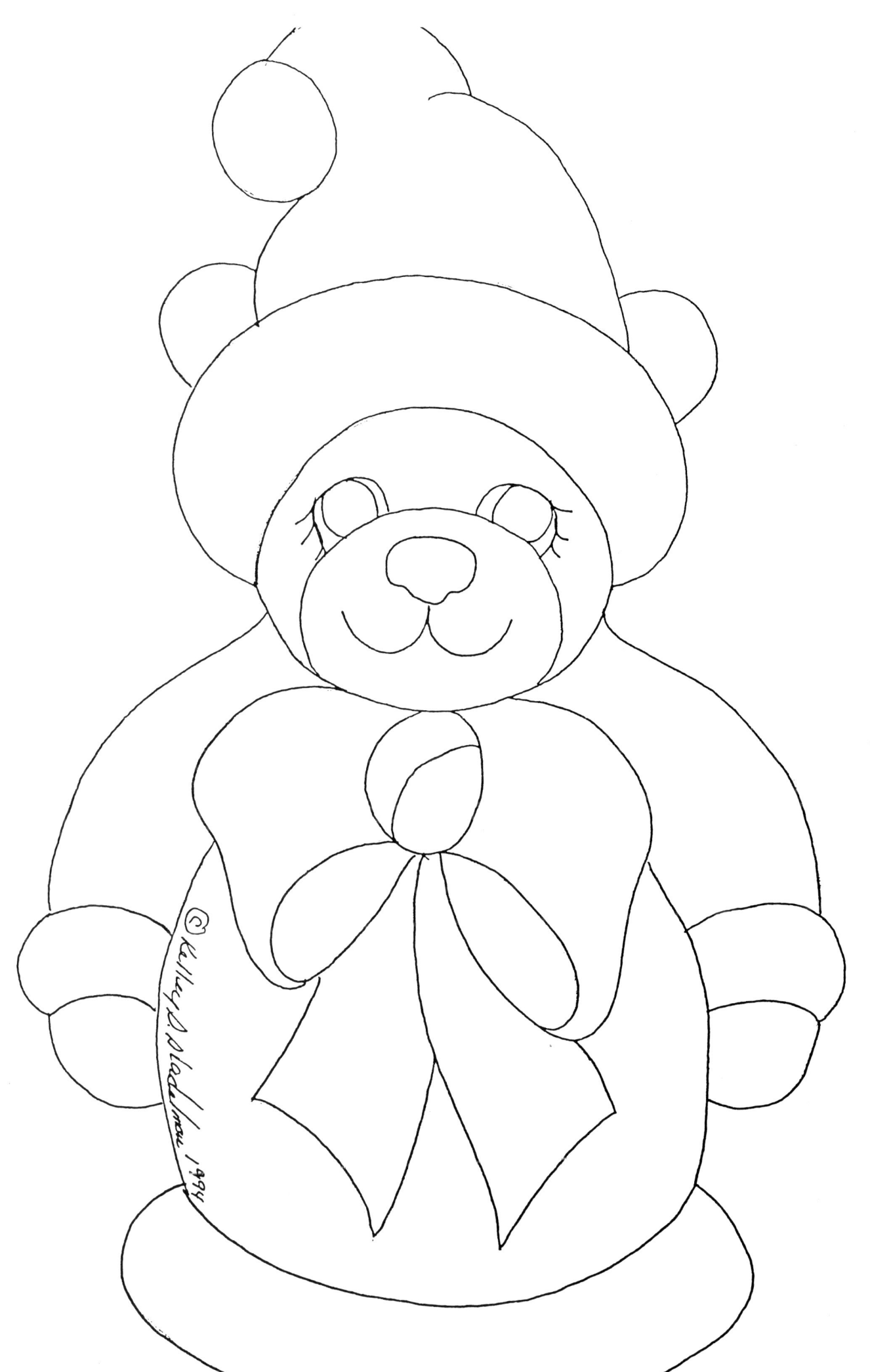

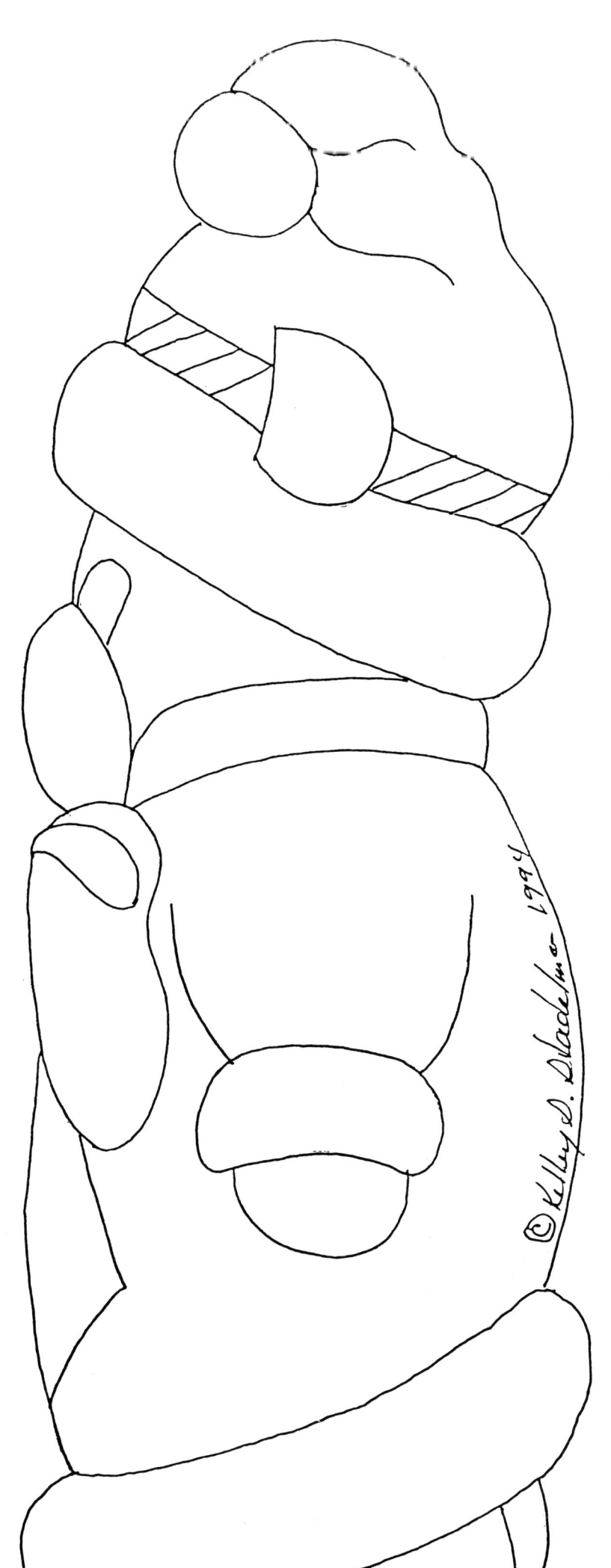

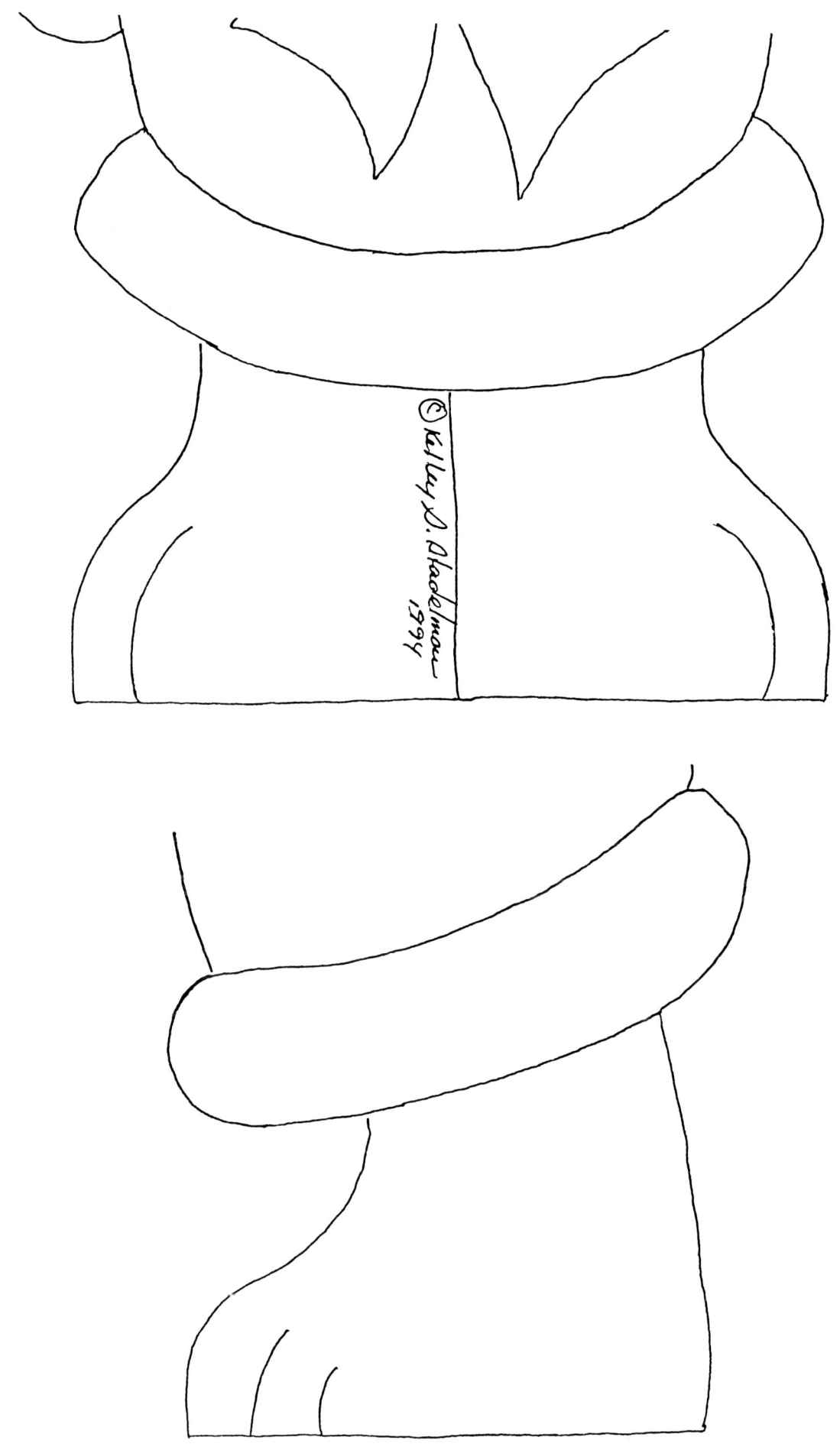

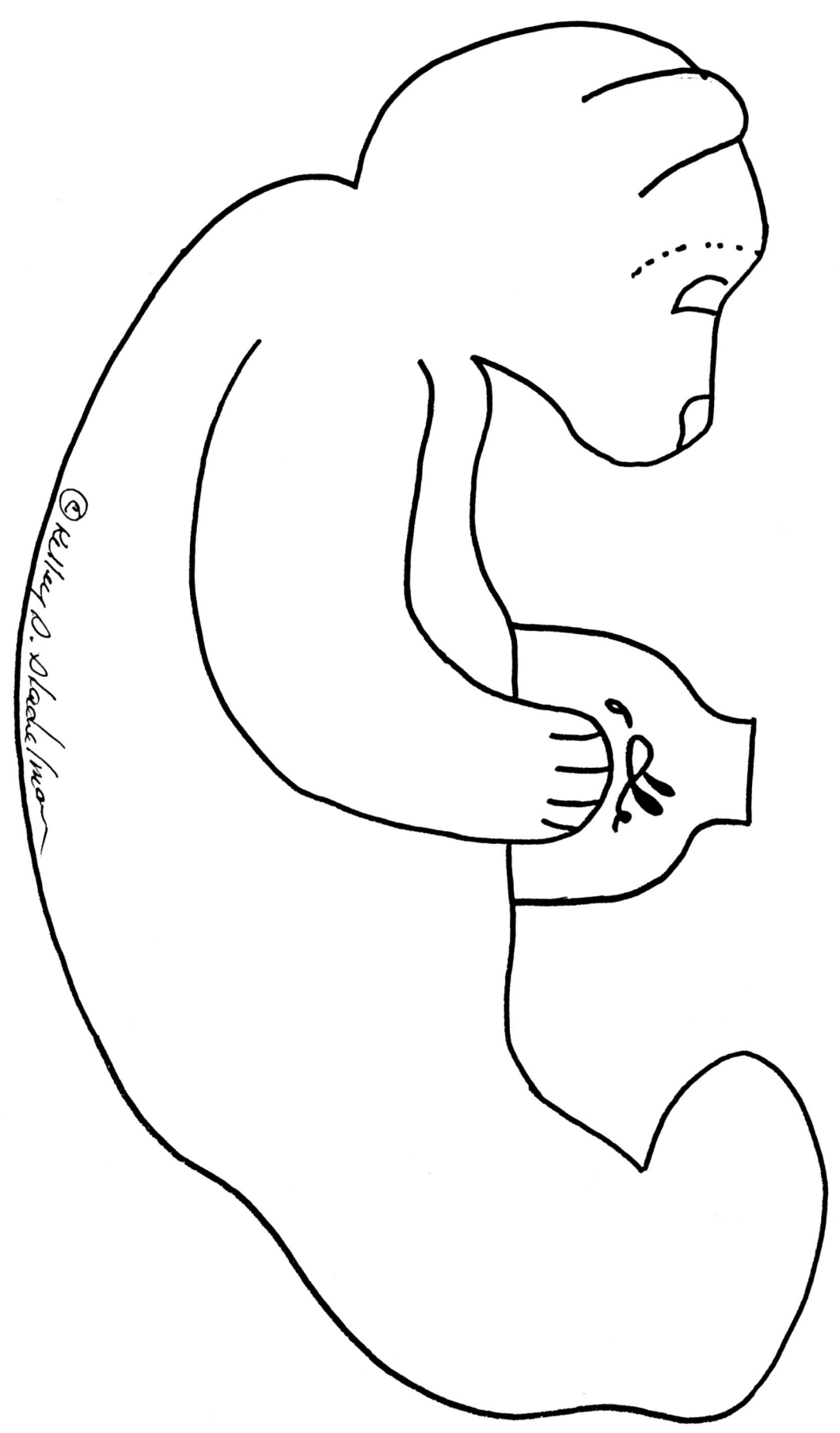

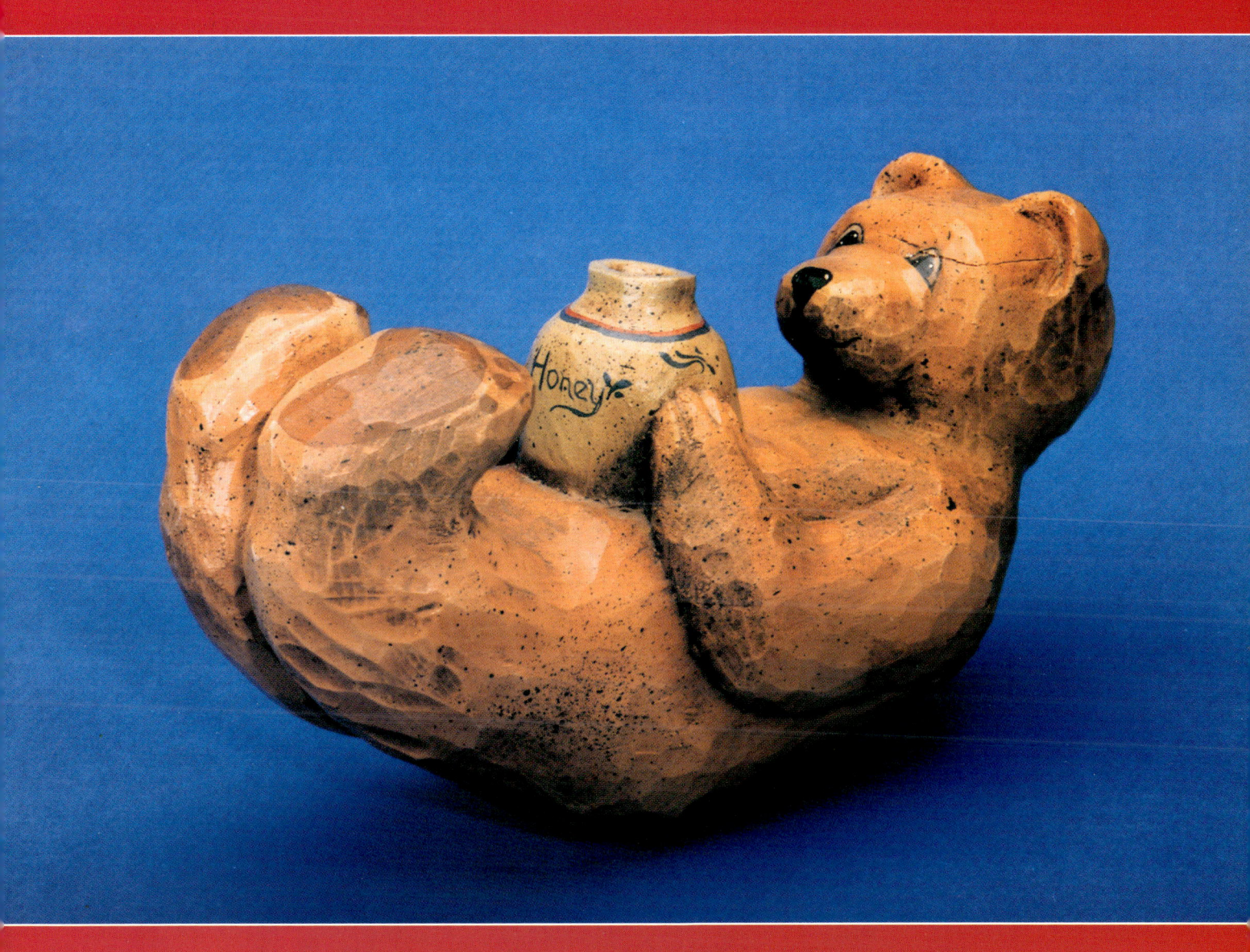

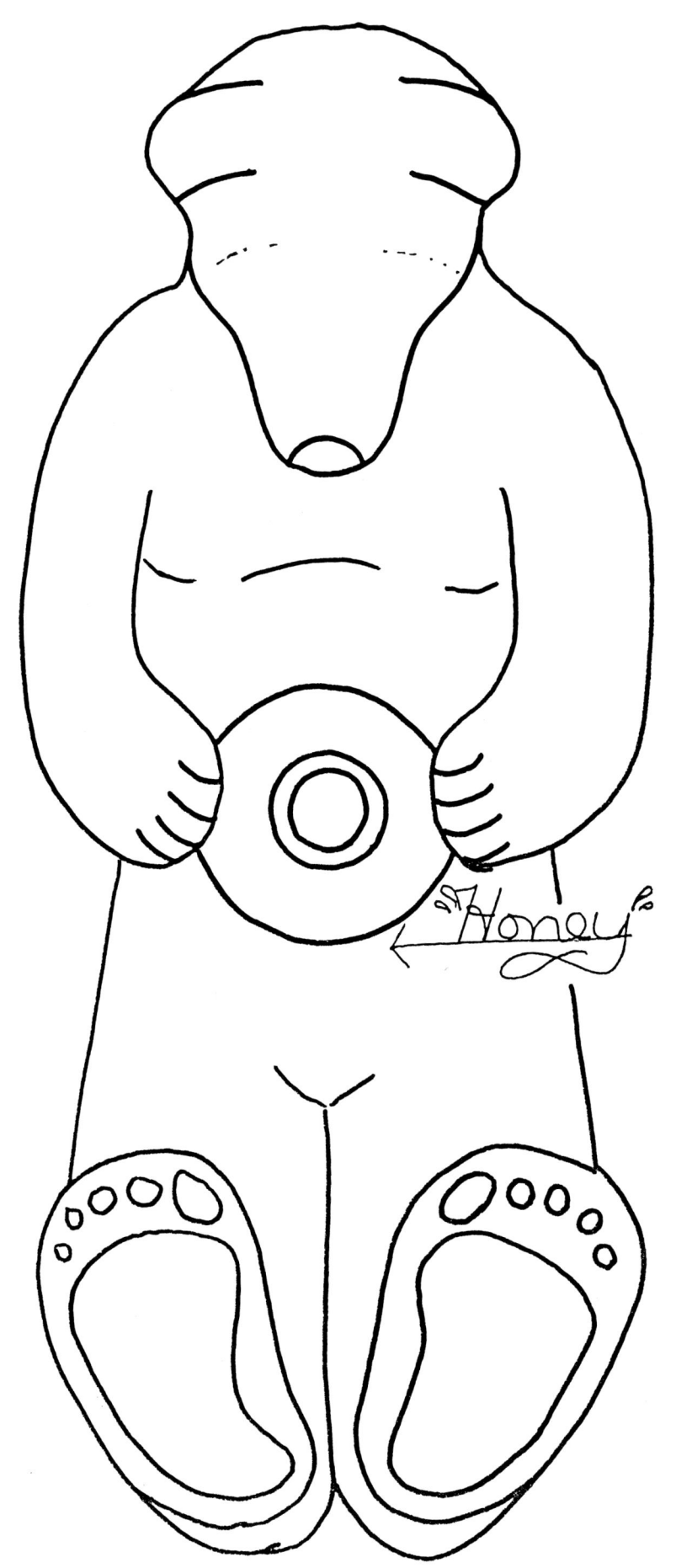

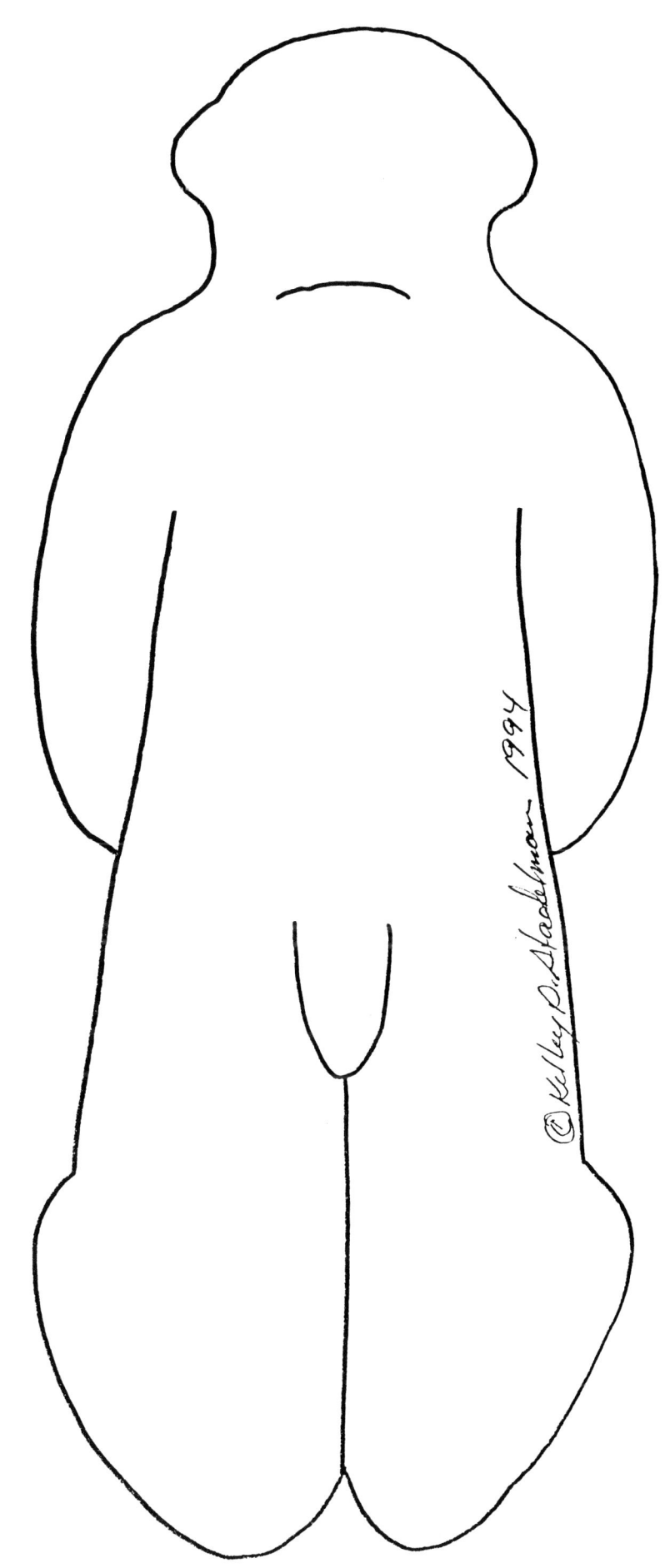

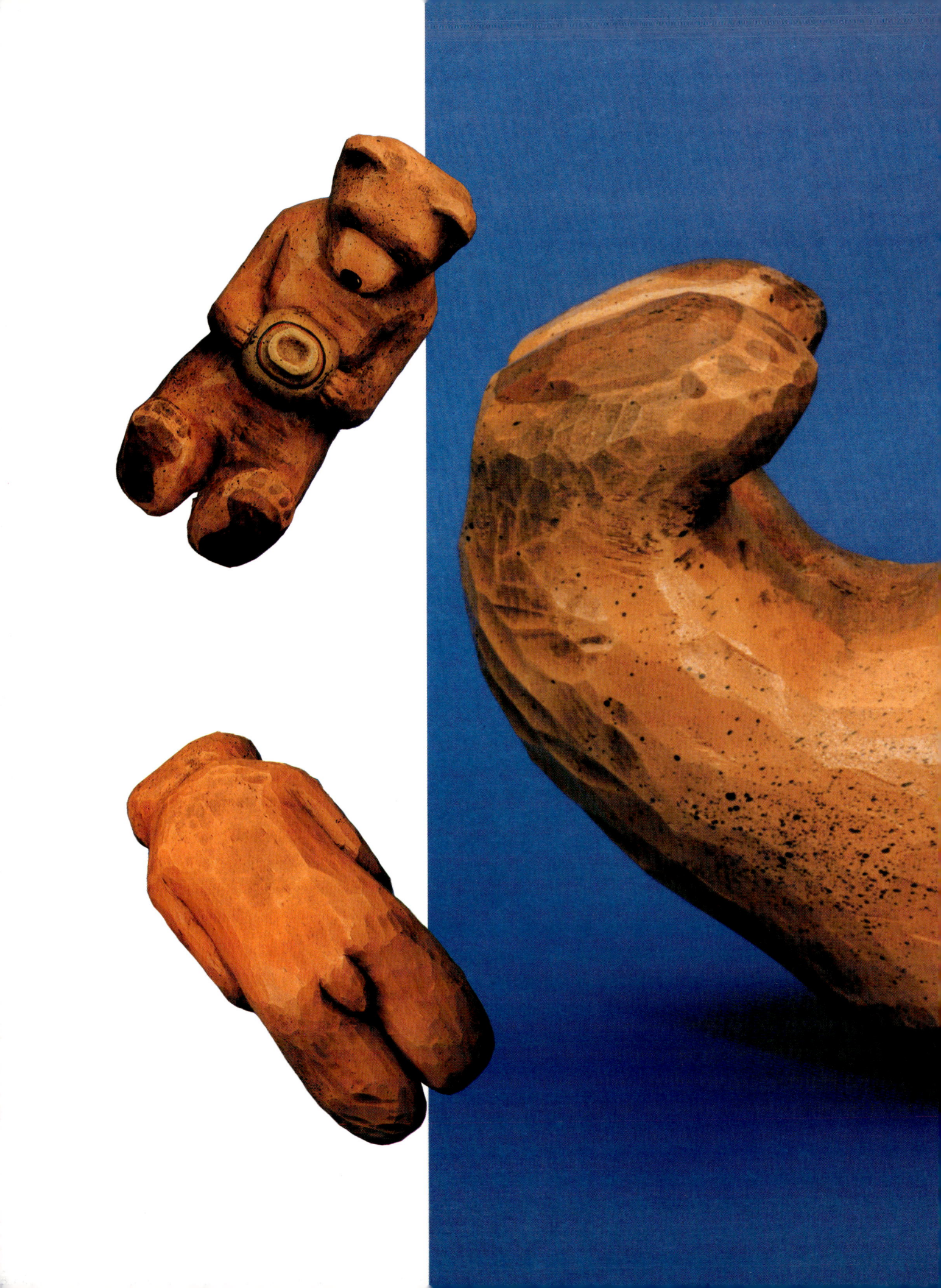

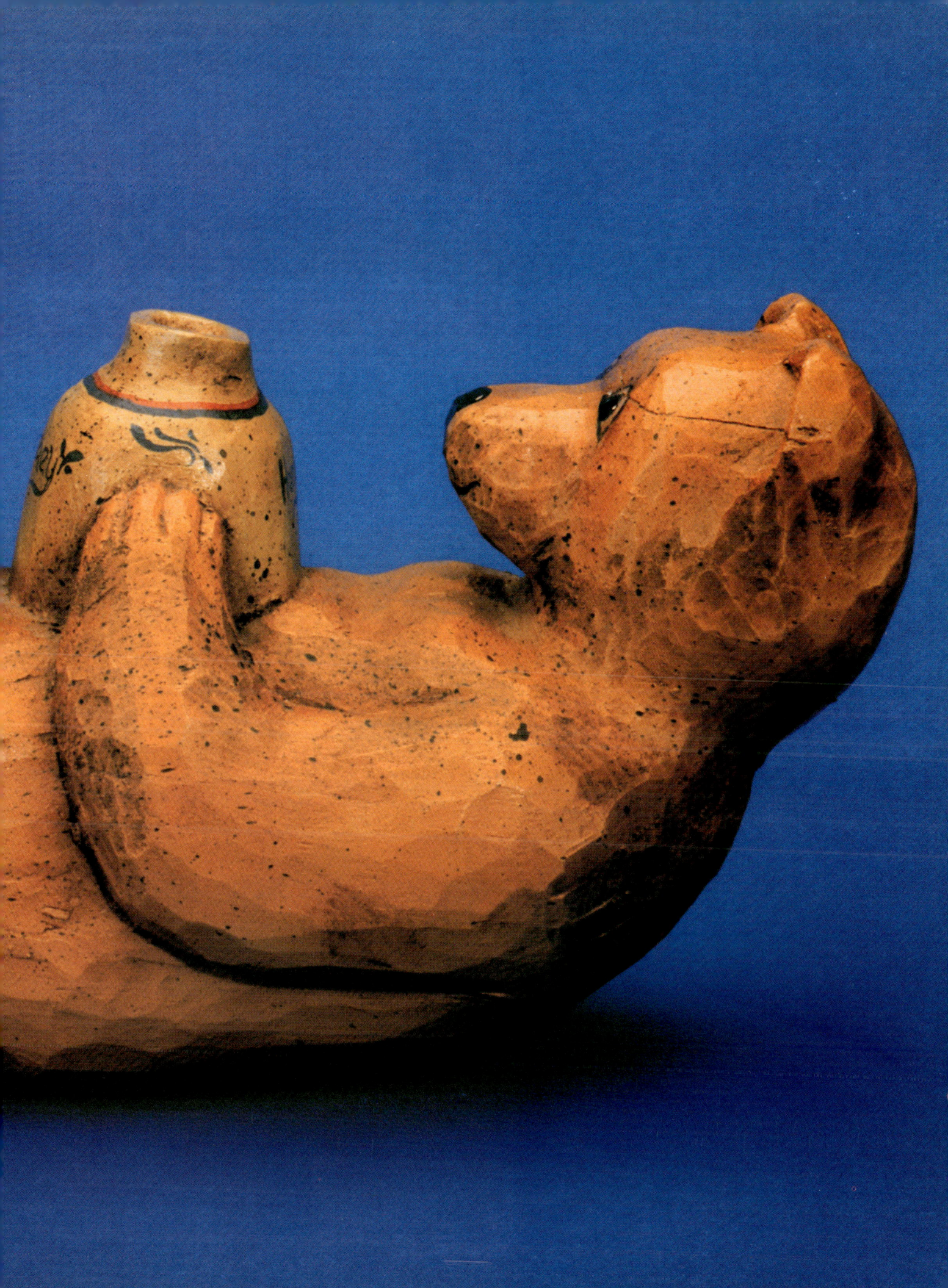

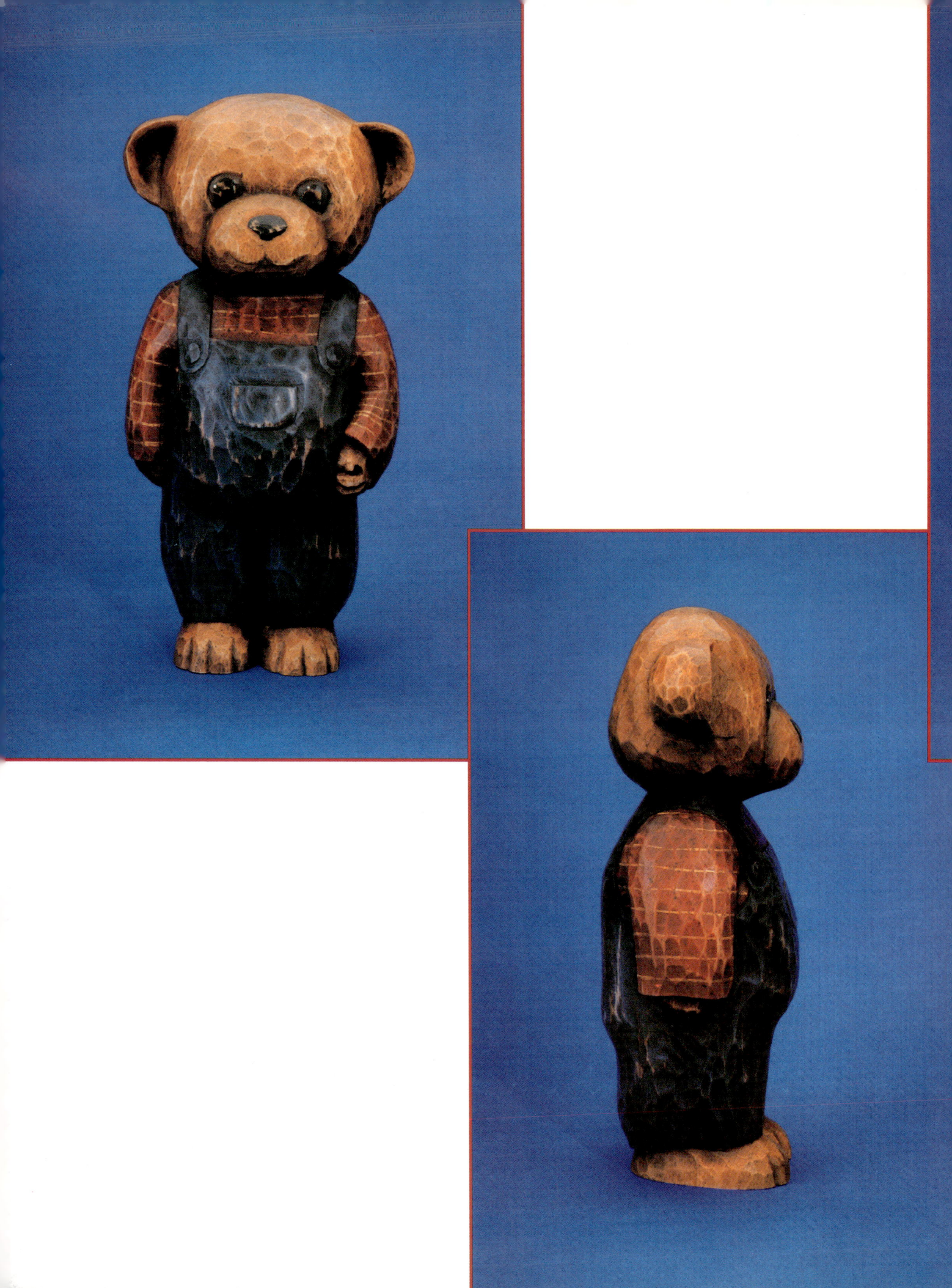

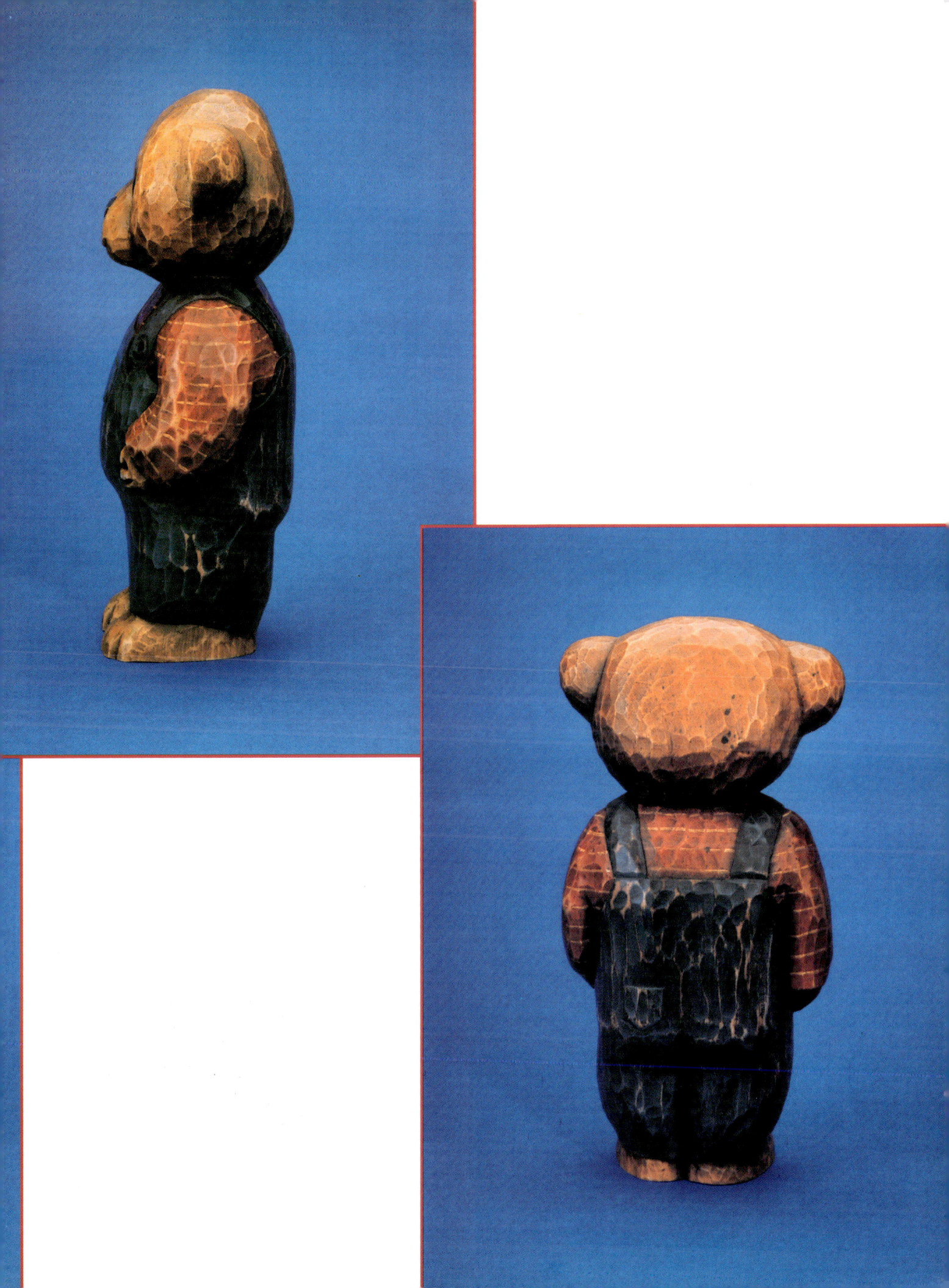

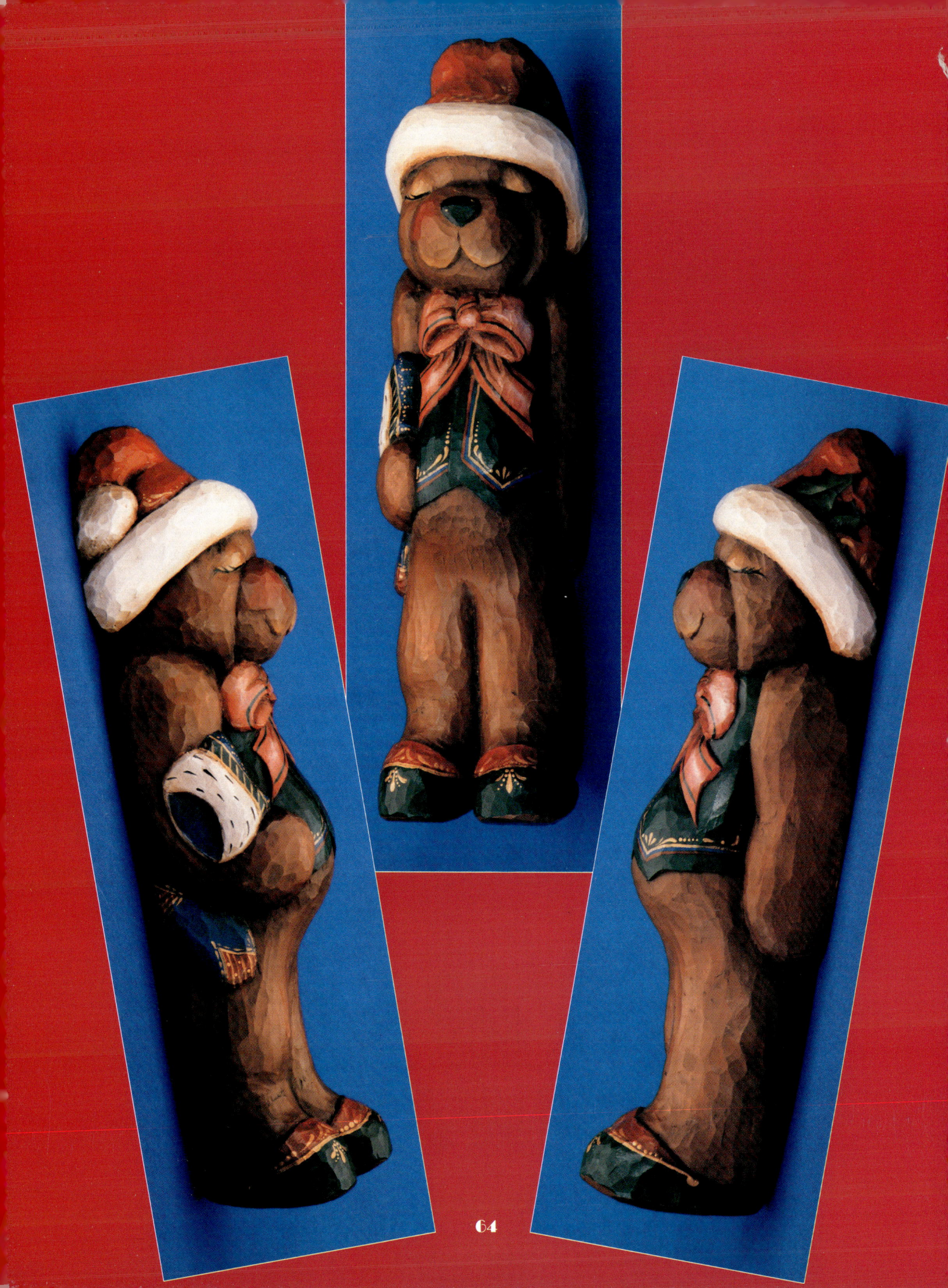